HE DID IT AGAIN!

More Miracles, Blessings and Chuckles

BETTY SHARRER

Betty Sharrer

MICK★ART
PRODUCTIONSLLC
PUBLISHING
www.mickartproductions.com

As I began to sort my messy jumbled pile of thoughts
& notes (some I could barely read myself), I asked the Lord if
I should even bother. He brought into my life a lovely
& talented young lady named DeAnna; and then He gave her
the additional measure of skill, patience and wisdom needed
to prepare my first book, "He Did It"...and now this second book,
"He Did It Again." I've heard that "gratitude is happiness,
doubled by wonder."
I'm truly grateful for so many things, a list long enuff to fill
a dozen big fat books, but for the moment I'll mention just two-
DeAnna & the Lord fill me with gratitude, happiness and wonder.
How else could a 91 year old retired sewing teacher
(who can't even type) write a book...no, two books?
Thank you DeAnna. Thank you Lord!

To contact Betty Sharrer call: 989-792-9545

ISBN: 978-0-9827000-9-9

Published by
Mick Art Productions, LLC
Email: mickmcart@gmail.com
www.mickartproductions.com

PRINTED IN THE UNITED STATES OF AMERICA

TABLE OF CONTENTS

INTRODUCTION PLUS

For decades people have teased me about my habit of collecting things---but wait...I don't collect stamps like my husband Bob did. I don't collect teapots like my Mother did, & some folks even collect cars. No, I have, for hundreds of years, (not really – I'm only 91) collected interesting things that other people have said or written. Many people have asked me WHY? To tell the truth, I never really knew why, till now! You see, I simply want to share all these treasures. As our kids usta' say, "We're Sharrers so we share."

These ideas & quotes are things I've been collecting all my life. You may find some will touch you where you live, others won't appeal to you. But I'm confident that you'll understand why I couldn't let them become extinct.

Also, I've added more of my TRUE STORIES of things that really happened to us, in us, & around us. As the old saying goes, "God will only give it to us if HE can get it through us...unto others."

History, I feel, always seems to be filled with the dates of wars, deaths & tears. I'd like my tales to be filled with help & kindness & memories of miracles, blessings & chuckles – Lots of them.

So, grab your reading glasses, find a comfy seat, bury your fone so we won't be interrupted, & let's start out with some of my collection of **WIT and WISDOM.**

LIFE'S BOOK

No matter what else you are doing
From cradle days through to the end
You are writing your life's secret story –
Each day sees another page penned.
Each month ends a thirty page chapter,
Each year means the end of a part –
And never an act is misstated.
Or even one wish to the heart.

Each day when you wake, the book opens,
Revealing a page clean and white –
What thoughts and what words and what doings
Will cover its pages by night?

God leaves that to you – you're the writer –
And never a word shall grow dim,
Till the day you write the word, "Finish"
And give back your life's Book to Him.

Unknown

HUGS

It's wondrous what a hug can do.
A hug can cheer you when you're blue.

A hug can say, "I love you so,"
Or, "Oh, I hate to see you go."

A hug is, "Welcome back again,"
And, "Great to see you! Where've you been?"

A hug can soothe a small child's pain
And bring a rainbow after rain.

The Hug! There's just no doubt about it—
We scarcely could survive without it!

A hug delights and warms and charms.
It must be why God gave us arms.

Hugs are great for fathers and mothers,
Sweet for sisters, swell for brothers.

And chances are your favorite aunts
Love them more than potted plants.

Kittens crave them. Puppies love them.
Heads of state are not above them.

A hug can break the language barrier
And make your friends so much merrier.

No need to fret about your store of 'em;
The more you give the more there's more of 'em.

So stretch those arms without delay
And GIVE SOMEONE A HUG TODAY!!!!

We are the adjectives pointing to, & describing the noun Jesus—
to all who do, or do not, know HIM

My face in the mirror isn't wrinkled or drawn.
My furniture is dusted, the cobwebs are gone.
My garden is lovely; so is my lawn.
Don't think I'll ever put my glasses back on.

BEAUTIFUL ONE-LINERS:

1. Give God what's right—not what's left.
2. Man's way leads to a hopeless end—God's way leads to an endless hope.
3. A lot of kneeling will keep you in good standing.
4. Don't put a question mark where God puts a period.
5. When praying, don't give God instructions—just report for duty.
6. Don't wait for six strong men to take you to church.
7. We don't change God's message—His message changes us.
8. When God ordains, He sustains.
9. Exercise daily—walk with the Lord.
10. Never give the devil a ride. He always wants to drive.
11. Nothing else ruins the truth like stretching it.
12. Compassion is difficult to give away because it always keeps coming back
13. He who angers you controls you.
14. Worry is the darkroom in which negatives can develop.
15. God doesn't call the qualified. He qualifies the called.

ALL I REALLY NEEDED TO KNOW, I LEARNED FROM NOAH'S ARK!

1. Don't miss the boat.
2. Don't forget that we're all in the same boat.
3. Plan ahead. It wasn't raining when Noah built the Ark.
4. Stay fit. When you're 600 years old, someone might ask you to do something REALLY big & important.
5. Don't listen to critics; just get on with what has to be done.
6. Build your future on high ground.
7. For safety's sake, travel in pairs.
8. Two heads are better than one.
9. Speed isn't always an advantage; the snails were on board with the cheetahs.
10. When you're stressed, float awhile.
11. Remember the Ark was built by amateurs; the Titanic was built by professionals & experts.
12. Remember the woodpeckers inside are a bigger threat than the storm outside.
13. No matter the storm, when you're with God, there's always a rainbow waiting!

MEN think computers should be referred to as females, just like ships, because:

1. No one but the Creator understands their internal logic.
2. The language they use to communicate with other computers is incomprehensible to everyone else.
3. The message "Bad command or file name" is about as informative as "If you don't know why I'm mad at you, I'm certainly not going to tell you."
4. Your smallest mistakes are stored in long-term memory for later retrieval.
5. As soon as you make a commitment to one, you find yourself spending half your paycheck on accessories for it.

WOMEN think computers should be referred to as male. Here's why:

1. They have a lot of data, but they are still clueless.
2. They are supposed to help you solve problems, but half of the time, they ARE the problem.
3. As soon as you commit to one, you realize if you had waited a little longer, you could have obtained a better model.
4. In order to get their attention, you have to turn them on.
5. A big power surge will knock them out for the rest of the night.

––––––––

Technology won't have justified itself until it can devise a machine to take the place of the old-fashioned handyman, or someone to shorten your pants.

––––––––

Television is a communications medium. It's called that because most of what you see on it is neither rare nor well done.

––––––––

If someone asks you who you are, what do you say? Can you name the 10 events in your life that make you YOU? What major decisions truly changed Your life? WHY?

———————

Words we use to describe others reveal the kind of a person we are. If we are courteous, we show courtesy in the use of our words and how we speak them. If we are rude, we interrupt others with words used in an ill-mannered impolite way. If we are thoughtless, lack of tact shows in our choice of words. We may use words to pry into or run the affairs of others.

———————

God intervenes when His people intercede.

———————

God's favorite word is COME.

———————

Our lives and the lives of others are revealed in our words. Radio, television, magazines and newspapers are some forms of communication which reveal the lives of persons to us via words. The influence exerted by words on our lives is continuous. Our opinions, our desires, our tastes, our perspective are determined by words.

———————

Words may serve us also. Our thoughts may become words. We influence others by our words. Our words attract or repel people or things. We bore, stimulate, restrict, encourage, forbid, entertain by our words. We may produce happiness or sadness by our choice of words.

———————

A cynic knows the price of everything but the value of nothing.

———————

Treasures in Heaven are laid up, as treasures on the earth are laid down.

"I SCREAM, YOU SCREAM, WE ALL SCREAM FOR ICE CREAM"

Growing up in Detroit had its advantages. I've never ever met anyone else who visited a store with a large sign that clearly said, "All the ice cream you can carry for a quarter."

Can you imagine the daddies with lotsa' kids who were thinking, "Wow, all my kids can have all the ice cream they want...Let's go!" Families stood in long lines. Many of them brought those large old fashioned oval laundry tubs. Some brought big round ones, all with handles on each side.

The daddies happily declared, "Fill it up!" As they held the big handles, in eager anticipation. They were shocked, when the employees first asked, and then checked, to see if it had been properly cleaned, before they added the lovely creamy treasure. Vanilla was the only choice.

Second; the huge machine oozed that lovely luscious stuff till it was about two inches deep in that long empty pan.

Third; the employee loudly demanded (not suggested) "Carry it to the door & back." It was about thirty feet. The area was roped off...a cleared path, and no one understood the process till each daddy had to walk it, both ways, carrying their huge containers, with only two inches of ice cream in the bottom. Then it had three inches, & then it had four inches. As I remember, most daddies made three trips & couldn't carry anymore.

The kids jumped up & down & whistled & shrieked, "More Daddy, more!" Even if it was someone else's daddy. Some children stood wide-eyed & silent with their fingers crossed. Then finally, they had to admit their limit & head for home.

A few young fellas tried to show off for their girlfriends. They probl'y had boasted how much they'd bring home to impress the parents, or other guys at the picnic.

I often wondered if it was still cold, when they got home. Ours always was.

Down the street was another large factory type building with a huge glass front. It resembled a used car sales room. Their big sign announced, "All the Vernor's Ginger Ale you can drink for a nickel."

The huge wooden vats in the back room were amazing. If we kids hung around long enough, the employees would urge us to sing or dance or whistle, & we got all the ginger ale free. Back then, we all loved Detroit.

ALLERGIES

When a six year old coughs all night, the procedure today is a lot different than it was in 1929. The entire nation was worried about banks closing & men jumping out windows, but my Mom was busy trying to stop my coughing.

She decided that lying in bed caused it, so she had me sit up, wrapped in blankets, beside the big coal stove, in our dining room. How could she know that dry heat made the problem worse?

No one spoke of allergies. Not many people knew & understood them, at that time. In fact, they can still be a big mystery & serious problem, today.

There was never money for doctors, but finally, my coughing was too severe, & home remedies for colds were useless, so the doctor visit was a must. He suggested a few foods to avoid, & urged moist heat, which helped a little.

As a teenager, in my job at Bell Telephone Company, I obviously used my voice. Every spring, when the cottonwood trees bloomed & blew their fuzzy-fluff everywhere, my voice disappeared. I had to work in a voiceless area of tandem boards.

In 1943, I married Bob & went to Texas with him. The allergies lessened there.

In 1954, Bob's job as manager of the Winkleman's store moved us to Saginaw, Michigan. We soon learned why Saginaw is known as "Sinus Valley." One night I was rushed to the Emergency Room. It took several hours, plus a variety of treatments & medications before I could breathe & swallow.

An allergy specialist, after I took all the tests, gave me a 3 x 5 file card completely filled with typewritten words. It took me a moment to understand why. Those were the things I was allergic to...and must avoid. Apples, wheat, lettuce, tuna & other types of fish, eggs, Kentucky Blue Grass, thistle, and my old nemesis, Cottonwood trees...they were just part of that scary list. How do you avoid things that surround us daily? I asked if I'd "out grow" allergies. The doctor's skeptical glance & his comment, "Highly unlikely, with this long list!" said it all.

At first, the allergy shots were twice a week. Then once a week, & finally, once a month, for several years. On our frequent train trips for thirty day vacations, I had the shot the day before we left & took the serum with me, packed in dry ice. I was warned to locate doctors to give me the injections, as needed. What a nuisance!

Several years later, as I arrived at the Bible Study prayer group one

Friday morning, a friend commented, "Betty, I hope you feel better than you look!"

"No...I really don't. I feel like they're taking my blood pressure around my forehead. Sinus pain or allergies, who knows," I moaned.

"Have you prayed about it?" he asked.

"OF COURSE I've prayed," I answered, rather hurt & insulted by his questions.

"Well, I mean...Well, I guess I asked the wrong question. Have you ever told it to go, in the name of Jesus?" he asked hesitantly.

If he had spoken to me in German or Greek, I would've understood just as clearly. What an odd question. My confusion showed on my face.

"Hey, folks, let's pray for Betty BEFORE we do the Bible study, OK?" Everyone gathered around, & put a chair in the center for me. At the many sessions I had attended previously, this was truly a FIRST.

As the leader opened his Bible & started to read passages of "Praise the Lord" type verses, the other folks did the same. They asked God to forgive all of us, because of what Jesus had done. His life, death & resurrection. The praises of that group were genuine & deeply sincere; my first experience of that kind of reverence, and joy, and expectancy.

Then the leader asked me "Do you believe that God is able to do anything? Do you accept Him not only as Savior & Lord, but also as our Deliverer?" "Oh yes!" I answered instantly.

"Will you repeat after me all the things I say...if you agree with them?" the leader asked, as everyone silently watched.

"Of course!" I quietly shouted. (Is that possible? Well, I did it anyway).

The first few statements were basic & easy to repeat. "Jesus, thank You for loving me & dying for me, to free me from the presence & power & punishment of sin. I rejoice that You came back to life, and are with us now after we accept You as Savior. We, no, I, want You to be the Lord of my life, and now, I want to witness & experience You as my Deliverer."

That was all valid & familiar, but then some newer ideas were spoken.

"Satan, get out of my life! Get out of my body! Jesus defeated you at the cross. All allergies must go & not return. I never ever accept allergies back again. In the powerful name of Jesus I command all allergies to leave forever. Thank you Father, for giving wisdom to the doctors for their help thus far. Now help them to know when no more allergy shots are needed. In the eternal name of Jesus, Amen."

I repeated every word, gladly, even tho' I was not as certain as the

9

others seemed to be. Perhaps it was their faith I was clinging to.

After two more shots, a month apart...the allergy specialist asked the same questions he always had, & decided to wait two months before the next one, "depending on what happens." He also added, he'd wait a while before ordering more serum.

I never had another allergy shot, nor ever needed one. Praise the Lord! He did it!

Awhile later, our country was threatened with Swine Flu (I believe that was the name of it) & everyone was urged to have Swine Flu Shots. All over the country empty stores were used to administer them, to thousands of people.

Bob had never been a bossy husband, so when he told me to go get one of the shots, I decided I'd better go. At the entrance of the long line of folks waiting to go in, was a big sign saying something like: "Important warning! The serum is made from (or with) eggs. If you are ALLERGIC to eggs, notify the staff." This was it. If I am truly delivered I will be fine. Am I truly & totally delivered? I took the shot!

No problem. Praise God! He did it again.

BASEBALL GAMES

Some people wonder why I don't get excited by the current ball games on T.V. They're always shocked to hear, "I'm soooo old I remember getting in to watch the big games at Tiger Stadium for a dime!"

My Dad had to work for two whole weeks, plus overtime, for the city of Detroit, to earn $10.00 in SCRIP. For those who don't know, that is sorta' like "Play Money." It could only be used for food, rent, gasoline & shoes, only essentials, so it left nothing at all for fun.

Daddy usta' say, "C'mon, Babe, let's go & spend our dimes." Mom handed me a huge bag of popped corn, (which wouldn't be allowed inside the park in today's world) and we truly did get in for 10¢ each. It was the seventh inning "stretch." Daddy declared that was the best part of the game, anyway.

Available seats were usually just above the dug-out or bullpen. The players teased & joked with us, as they returned from the field. One day, after Babe Ruth hit a home run, the ball was returned to him. He turned to me grinning, & said, "Hey there, li'l redhead...do you want this flying magic ball? Here, let me sign it for ya!" I was excited, of course & even hugged him. Another day, Hank Greenburg did the same thing, & tossed it gently to me. If I had known how famous they would both become...but then it didn't mean much to a six year old, just fun.

If I had one of those autographed balls, I could probly' buy a new car (or two). I recently read that it may cost about $200. to take a family of four to watch the Tigers play ball. My precious memories of homemade popcorn and 10¢ ball games are far richer.

Those two special baseballs were probably chewed up by Ring, the neighbor's big black & white dog, who chewed up everything he found. Neither Ring nor I had any idea of the value of two baseballs.

Babe Ruth & Hank Greenburg never knew how much they blessed that little six year old & her Daddy, nor did they even suspect that 84 years later they'd still be remembered as "nice guys."

I DIDN'T KNOW HOW

Our kids & grandkids tease me about all of my stories...those in my first book "HE DID IT"...and the ones in this book, "HE DID IT AGAIN." The kids claim I started writing them when the Mayflower landed. That isn't true; I didn't start till after the Civil War ended.

There were notes & phrases & partial stories on the back of crumpled envelopes, even the torn half of a paper napkin. No one can explain where they were & why they were all submerged; buried under stacks of old greeting cards & other outdated "stuff."

As I sorted those stacks, Bob once asked, "Why doncha' just dump that whole pile in the trash? Is it worth your time to sort it? Here's a paper sack...shall I help you?"

When I found a $20 bill, a moment later, & then a restaurant gift card for $50 in another birthday card, Bob said, "OK—so it wasn't a waste of time."

But...all those chunks of stories...whatever should be done with them? I'd find a few words scribbled on a scrap of paper & wonder what to do with it.

Those "story starts" began to pile up, so I found a large reused envelope for them. Then they needed a manila folder. Later, as they oozed out of the folder, I found a shoe box. But, folded in that shape became less efficient so I located a boot box. All the while, wondering why am I keeping this junk? What good is it?

The major hold-up was a simple one... they were all scribbled in long hand, & no one would accept stories that were not typed. Many were barely legible, even to ME.

11

A friend, named Olive, had a book published. She was a brilliant lady who had taught nursing in college, so I assumed she was from a different planet than a non-typer like me. She insisted that I learn, gave me a typing lesson, & ordered me to practice.

Boy, did I practice! Our son-in-law drove all the way here from Iowa, to loan me his new electric typewriter. I practiced at least two or three hours every day for three months. That typewriter lived on the dining room table, so I'd have no excuse to skip the practice times, two or three times a day.

On the 89th day, I typed a simple short paragraph, made 17 glaring errors, put the cover on, and declared, "I do not type! I've given it my very best. That's it...no more!" The typewriter was returned to Iowa with deep gratitude, but a sense of finality. I do not type!

Dearly determined Olive insisted, "Betty, you could type if you really wanted to!" I went into dramatic detail about my futile attempts & failure. But, she refused to accept the idea.

My solution was, "Olive, I've sewed for you for years cuz you couldn't shorten your own skirts & coats, sooo—howsabout...I'll sew for you & you can type for me...OK?!!"

Shortly after that Olive became very ill & died.

Another friend with office skills, offered to type my stories. I gave her one. It looked beautiful, but had so many errors that my red pencil corrections made it look like it had measles. Another friend took a story to type, & lost it.

Another friend had a friend, who wanted to earn money for college, to prepare for the mission field. My comments were, "Feel free to make needed corrections, & I'm in no hurry."

When the story was finally returned to me, it was no longer MY story. There were not only corrections (which we later deemed NOT needed) but sentences were completely altered. Not my story.

Another friend offered to use the library computer, but I couldn't drive her over there & wait for her. So another attempt failed. How dismal.

All of those attempts took place several years before Bob's illness.

When Bob became totally dependant on me, I couldn't leave him alone for even five minutes. The Veterans Hospital supplied us with a helper who stayed with Bob for two hours a week so I could shop for groceries & do other errands. Of course, those silly old stories were buried by the day-to-day necessities.

Once in a while, Bob would ask me to share one of the stories to add a new wrinkle, or make minor changes in the ones relating to his military career. I was glad he helped me strive for accuracy. His silly sense of humor was a real bonus. Even after we had dated for over two years & were married nearly 70 years, I never got used to his ridiculously funny, but never hurtful, sense of humor; I just appreciated his nuttiness more & more.

Perhaps the stories, the humor, & the loving family we shared, are all parts of the fabulous memories that make up our lives, OUR STORY.

Everyone has a STORY, made up of dozens, no, hundreds, of little stories. We can enrich the lives of those around us sometimes, by sharing our stories.

But, back to the original topic, since no one would even read my un-typed or un-computered stories, they were literally on the shelf.

Let's go back still further. About eight years before all this happened, as I was standing in the shower one morning, planning my day, an amazing event took place; one I'll never ever forget.

Many folks sing in their shower, many plan their day. I was making a mental list of groceries, the bank, the gas station...when all of sudden I heard (there's no other way to describe it) a clear voice saying, "The title of the book will be "HE DID IT." What book?

I was stunned & bewildered, but obviously I will never forget it. However, I put it on HOLD, as I tended to my precious husband's needs.

So, here I am, back at my frustrating dilemma. What do I do with this box full of rough draft, hand written stories?

Now wait a minute; if God cares enough about my silly stories to call them a BOOK & give that book a name, maybe they're not so silly after all.

"Father, I treasure Your opinion. If You give me a name for them, why can't I get them typed or in condition for a publisher? This whole project is now completely in Your hands, where it should have been in the first place. Even tho' I prayed, I kept trying to help You...to do it my way. NO MORE. If there's to be a book, it's up to YOU, in Jesus' wise name. Amen."

Recently our granddaughter & her husband invited me to visit a different church with them. It was a beautiful building, friendly people, and good sermon. The next week I was visited by a member of that church, who I knew from our previous experience working together on blood drives. When she arrived, I had story papers spread all over the sofa & tables, trying to sort them. What a mess.

I was pleased to see her. Small talk ended in her questions about the papers all over the room. Briefly I told her about my stories, the title

God had given me, & my inability to type.

"My daughter types. Call & ask her if she's available & willing to help," my friend offered. I called her daughter, & she lovingly agreed.

Not only was she willing, but sweetly & truly capable. She knew (or learned) everything needed. I did not need to know how...Praise the Lord! For, when I quit struggling & trying to do it my way, & gave it completely to God, He did it!

He obviously knew when, who, & how. His timing is always PERFECT.
HE DID IT!

DATES

Growing up in crowded Detroit, it was a treat to get to parks & lakes. Bob & I met in our teens & dated for two years before we were married in 1943. We had no money so our dates were unusual by today's standards.

My Mom invited Bob to eat meals at our house quite often, & we rarely "ate out." One place we could afford, & loved to go, was Hale's Drug Store. The chocolate malted milk they served was in that big tall silver container, but it was full to the top. They swirled real whipped cream inside two large glasses...& that container filled both glasses TWICE for 15¢! Bob never ever called me a cheap date, but it seems to qualify. Today $4.00 wouldn't come close for one, & we got two for our 15¢. Unbelievable, isn't it?

Some evenings we spent in a Record Shop. The purpose was to take six records at a time into the small booth, to decide which ones we chose to buy. The booths were about four feet square with a bench on one wall, & a record player & shelf on one wall. The sweet man who owned the place knew we intended to buy nothing, but he grinned, & pretended we were normal customers, as we sat & played his records for hours & hours.

Once we toured Detroit's famous Belle Isle. In the center is a big lovely aquarium in a huge glass building. The sun streamed down on the zillions of fish all colors, all sizes, all types. One large gold fish really looked like an electric light when the sun shone on it. Bob said, rather loudly, "See, Hon, that's how you look in a crowd."

I was so embarrassed; I burst out of the big glass building, past all of the people, & ran crying to the car. Poor Bob! He had a terrible time trying to convince me he meant it as a compliment. I had hated my red hair all my life & I was hard to convince. I had a lot to learn, & so did Bob. He was 19 & I was 17.

We rode our bicycles all over town regularly, & took picnics to wherever we'd find a patch of grass. To rent canoes cost a dollar, & we saved up to do that.

We were thrilled to receive an invitation to visit a cottage on Lake Orion, & a ride both ways, about 40 miles from Detroit, I think. The owners of the lovely old cottage were elderly friends of Bob's family.

When we arrived at the top of a large hill, I was excited to run up & down & up & down again on the long flight of steps made of huge old logs, submerged, partially buried in ivy & tree roots & fern. Bob & our hosts laughed aloud at my delight.

Our hosts decided to delay lunch as Bob & I were eager to get into the lake for a swim. To "wait an hour" after lunch would be torture—& that's what everyone expected in those days.

In ten seconds we were in our bathing suits & running down those gorgeous old wooden steps. The cottage was not even visible from the water's edge, the hill was so high.

I couldn't swim, so we were told where to swim & what area to avoid, for safety. We giggled & splashed & stayed close to shore.

And then the bottom dropped out. I choked & screamed & thrashed about in terror. As I rose to the surface, I tried to yell, but I could no longer make a sound, I was too full of water.

Bob grabbed me & tried to help, but he was not prepared, nor trained, to handle my panic. I must have passed out.

When I woke up, I was lying face down on the sandy beach, water gushing from my mouth. What a shock! Bob sat beside me choking & coughing.

The strap of my one piece, modestly cut bathing suit had broken when I was dragged into the boat that brought us to shore. As a result, the top half of my bathing suit was doubled under & I was uncovered from the waist up. Good that I was awake & could adjust the suit before I sat up. That seems trivial now, but I must've been "out of it" to allow such a situation.

Because the house was so high above the lake, no one up there heard my screams. They weren't aware of our plight till our host came down to call us for lunch.

The mystery that was never solved was...who was the man in the boat who dragged me into his boat, & threw Bob a rope to get us back to shore? Bob tried to describe him & his small boat (only large enough for two people) but he was too upset to remember much.

Our hosts had lived there for decades & knew all their neighbors. They tried to find the man to thank him for truly saving our lives, but never found him. No one knew him.

We all say we've never seen an angel, & that sounds realistic. But, we can't find a better explanation. We're still open to ideas.

Hebrews 1:14 "Are they not all ministering spirits, sent forth to minister for them who shall be heirs of salvation?"

Earlier that day in Detroit, Bob's Dad was working, & mid morning his work was interrupted by thoughts of Bob and me. He called Bob's Mom (at her job) to ask about us. They agreed to pray for us, not knowing where we were. When they learned later that evening, what had occurred, they were shocked. His Mom burst into tears & called me at my home to tell me. My Mom cried too, and so did I...tears of joy!

Whatever happened...GOD did it!

PRICELESS GIFTS

"A hundred years ago," as my sister, Helen, & I grew up in big busy Detroit, we were always excited & eager to visit the fabulous events planned for that magical day, the Friday after Thanksgiving. Hudson's huge store was still downtown, & even though it took long bus rides to get there, we couldn't wait to see their fairy land with lights, & glitter, & mystical decorations everywhere. Long, long lines of kids & parents waited for hours to visit Santa Claus. (He must've been exhausted, sitting there & smiling sweetly to all those kids, who pretended to be good).

At that time, our Daddy brought home only $10.00 in scrip for two weeks work. It could only be used for rent, food, & other necessities. Soooo, our thrills of delight were far different than most of the other kids. They breathlessly told Santa their wishes & desires; of course, truly expecting to find them all under their Christmas trees. We didn't.

Our goal was to find new & clever ideas for things we could MAKE for others, with no money.

Now that's a noble (almost impossible) task. We were terrified, but determined, and so eager.

One of those years, we saw a cleverly creative game. (Not new now, but new to us then). So, the next day we searched for all of the stuff needed to duplicate it. We coaxed a store keeper for a big box that a kitchen stove had been packed in, to make a clown's face.

Daddy made the three & a half foot square box sturdy, & slanted, at just the right angle. Then he helped us cut out large circles for the clown's eyes, a triangle for his nose, & a crescent mouth.

We gathered leftover paints from neighbors & friends to make that

16

happy, silly clown as colorful as possible. We found some yarn scraps & even unraveled an old orange & brown sweater to make his wild hair. Gramma helped us make a funny ruffled collar from worn out pajamas.

OK...that completed, Grampa suggested we might get some 'throwaway' beans at the local company that packaged rice & beans. I was eight & my sister, Helen, was thirteen. She asked the man in the office for any beans "they didn't need." He smiled at Grampa, & brought us a five pound bag of assorted beans & rice they cleaned up each day at closing time,...FREE!

Gramma supplied us with fabric scraps, all sizes & colors, to make a dozen bean bags to throw through the holes in the clown's face. That's where & when I learned to sew on Mom's old treadle (non-electric) sewing machine.

Nearly done...but we agreed it needed a RULES CHART on the back of the big box. We carefully printed (in pencil first, of course) then in ink:

- 5 points for the mouth
- 10 points for the left eye
- 15 points for the right eye
- 20 points for the nose
- EXTRA 50 points for all four. Yes! Now it was finished.

Another year we begged empty thread spools, glued them together & painted them, for a big candle holder for Gramma & Grampa. One year we saved (all year) the small boxes that soap came in, & made a long train, with engine & caboose, for Daddy.

The most fun was the year we carefully sliced (with Daddy's help) the toilet paper roles & paper towel cores (from all our friends) to make rings, which we then glued to tissue paper. It was a 'gorgeous' wall hanging for Momma.

Helen & I recently agreed, we can't remember what gifts we received those years, but we vividly remember the high tension thrills & fun we had making those free, but priceless gifts...plus the true, contagious joy on the faces of those who received them. Such giggles & hugs & fake humility!

As our three kids grew up, my husband managed a large retail store, & he became 'peopled out' after the big holiday seasons. But, we agreed, we wanted our kids to find their thrills, motivation, & memories to come from pleasing others, just as my parents taught.

We moved to a smaller city, where the big department store must have spent a small fortune to decorate their many huge windows with story book charm. Our family devoted many hours just sharing the creativity & joy of those delightful windows. And...actually, we never stopped seeking ideas for 'priceless gifts' we could make.

Those long lines near Santa Claus & the gorgeous, magical decorations are still exciting. Once in a while we even see something that displays the REAL meaning of Christmas. We are pleased that the gifts our kids made, & gave to others (with little or no money) remain more memorable than any of the more lavish ones they received.

After all, whose birthday is it, anyway?

When our adult daughter embroidered beautiful flowers on pillow cases for her Gramma, we were grateful that she still gives priceless gifts.

AFTER THE DANCE

Most everyone went to dances as a teenager. But, I think my memories are different than most others.

There were seven or eight couples of us, & always one or two adults. No matter whose parents they were, we all called them Mom & Dad.

In those days, we put three in the front seat, & three or more in the back seat of each of the three cars. Once we squeezed 18 teens & two adults in. Squeezed.

We attended three different schools, but all lived in the same neighborhood of big busy, noisy Detroit. We found it too hard to wait for Fridays.

The dances were held in a large Catholic school hall, with lotsa' Chaperones, & great music from phonograph records. Today's kids don't know about 78's & 45's.

That's where I became a true Jitterbug. My partners practiced throwing me over their heads...prob'ly cuz I weighed 89 pounds. We all won blue ribbons & fake gold-cups as prizes. Square dances were the most fun & even the chaperones liked to polka.

One night, as our three-car-caravan headed for home, Dad, in the lead car, took a surprise turn to take us up onto the long, high bridge that spanned the huge factories manufacturing cars, (Fords, I think).

All of our car windows went down simultaneously, in spite of the brisk October midnight air. We were enthralled by the clouds of billowing smoke, the amazing mysterious play of lights in that blackened, night sky. "Hey, look over there!"..."What's that big thing"..."Wow, so much smoke!"...Comments were yelled out every window, with exclamation points on every one. And then...two Police cars with flashing lights, rushed beside us, and our three cars became silent.

One policeman, with a loud distinct Irish brogue, asked, "S'matter folks, don't we have a color to suitya'? We have tried green yella' red, green yella' red, green yella' red...& you're still sitten' here. What color are ya' waitin' for?"

Barbara, the girl next to me, whispered, "He sounds just like Pat O'Brien!" But, the rest of us looked up to discover that we were "shur nuff" parked under traffic signals. OOPS!

It was up to THE DAD in our first car, to try to explain that all 19 of us had just left a school dance, we had only root-beer to drink, & we were sorry that we were "disturbing the peace" at 12:45 AM.

The four officers laughed out loud, & cautioned us with phony seriousness to, "Quiet down & go home to sleep it off!" They swiftly drove off, still laughing, & left us all dazed. That was a quiet ride home.

One summer night after the dance, one of our three cars wouldn't start, even with all of the young car experts, (& one Dad) trying to fix it. The two adults conferred privately, as we all stood around trying to "figger out" what to do to get help. That was 1939 BC...before Cell 'fones.

Finally, Dad & Mom offered a suggestion that would need 100% agreement. We were so eager to hear their idea.

"If you will all...ALL...raise your right hands & promise, on your word of honor, to be on your very best behavior, & to go straight,...STRAIGHT...home! NO detours, NO mischief, NO teasing...& all 16 of you will call us the very minute you get home; we will drive the other two cars home (& come back for the "sick" one, in the morning) AND, we'll let you dopey, silly, ignoramuses WALK home, together. You'll drop one off, & each one will call us as you arrive safely. You'll CALL us, right? Each one will call as soon as they get home!"

Our shouts of delight & promises could probly' be heard a mile away at our homes, I vividly remember walking eight abreast, down the center of the side streets, in two rows, holding hands & singing dumb songs (TOO LOUD).

It was hilariously silly & fun. When I think back my feet hurt (some of the kids carried their shoes), & my heart sings to think of all those Moms & Dads, and especially the two who accepted 16 phone calls at one or two in the morning. I wish we had thanked them more seriously, but I'm sure they knew. I wonder how they could've been so wise, so trusting, so loving, so patient, & so silly!

19

That should end this tale, but there's another silly part of it. Because I loved to dance, everyone was shocked when I married a wonderful man who did not dance. Bob was worth the sacrifice.

After 60 years together, on one of our frequent train trips to California, we visited my cousin Marie.

When she announced that we were going to a dinner dance, I expected Bob to react or to question. He didn't. I was secretly delighted.

After the lovely meal, we entered a large hall with a small band playing at one end. Circular tables were all around the room & Bob headed quickly to sit down. The music was great, old & new favorites. I asked Bob if he planned to dance. "I'm waiting for a slow one," he found a hesitant answer.

"Well Honey, the slow ones, you need to know what you're doin'... but the fast ones, you just jump around in time to the music...& no one cares if you know what you're doing!" Before my words hit the table, Bob grabbed my hand & we just kept dancing.

As we danced past the grandstand, Marie & her husband came close. She asked us, "How many years have y'all been married?" I shouted, "This was our 60th, and we still like each other." Bob laughed.

The bandleader heard us & asked, "How many years?" Marie told him, he stopped the music, cleared the floor of the nearly 100 couples, & the band started to play "The Anniversary Waltz." He said, "60 years, even in Michigan is nearly a miracle, but in California it really is one!" As Bob & I danced ALONE on that huge dance floor, it must've been quite an experience for his first dance. It was, and still is, PURE joy for me. We were married nearly 70 wonderful years...lotsa' joy, & my heart still dances.

GETTING FIRED MADE ME LAUGH

Shortly after Bob & I were married in 1943, the army moved us AGAIN. Actually we were sent to 14 different large & small towns in central Texas. One of those many apartments was actually part of a very big, very old house that was divided, so that three couples could share it.

We were happy to have what our friends called the best one-third of the newly painted old mansion. Houses of that type in San Francisco were often called "Painted Ladies" (or something poetic like that). We entered into a lovely living room that may have been called a parlor, in its day.

The rest of the place had happy & well coordinated colors...but...best of all, there was a big ole' upright piano in the front room. It looked very cozy & folks who knew about such things, said the piano "had a nice voice."

One day when I finished making the bed & doing dishes, I wondered how other "married ladies" can stand it! I was so used to working everyday, this just seemed too boring.

Then, I had an idea. It didn't take much effort to locate the only piano teacher in that little town & set up my twice weekly piano lessons. She said she'd expect me to practice a lot since I had no job & no kids.

So, I did. I practiced, at least twice a day, for more than an hour. That too became boring, but at least I had hopes of someday learning to play that old piano. Hours & hours of practice.

After about two months of diligent...& do I mean diligent...practice, one day, the sweet voiced, kindly teacher said, "Betty, we do need to talk. I know how hard you've worked. You've tried to fiercely practice to learn, BUT, let's be realistic, you are wasting your money & your time...& also my time. Dear, you'll never be a true piano player. Perhaps you should take up knitting or painting or photography, don't you agree?" It was such a relief to hear her say it, (so that I wouldn't be called a quitter), that I laughed out loud. Who else have you ever heard of that got fired by a piano teacher?

THE HAIRCUT

A teenage boy had just passed his driving test and inquired of his father as to when they could discuss his use of the car.

His father said he'd make a deal with his son: "You bring your grades up from a C to a B average, study your Bible, and get your hair cut. Then we'll talk about the car."

The boy thought about that for a moment, decided he'd settle for the offer, and they agreed on it.

After about six weeks his father said, "Son, you've brought your grades up and I've observed that you have been studying your Bible, but I'm disappointed you haven't had your hair cut."

The boy said, "You know, Dad, I've been thinking about that, and I've noticed in my studies of the Bible that Samson had long hair, John the Baptist had long hair, Moses had long hair – and there's even

strong evidence that Jesus had long hair."
You're going to love the Dad's reply:
"Did you also notice that they all walked everywhere they went?"
Pastor Dave Horton

ANSWERED PRAYER

I've heard that Mrs. Billy Graham once said, "I'm glad that God doesn't always say YES when He answers our prayers. I may have been married to three of the wrong men." God obviously knows what is best for us. Sometimes He sez "Yes"...Sometimes He sez "NO"...Sometimes He sez "Not yet"...Sometimes He sez, "What took you so long to ask me? I've been waiting & waiting for you to give this problem to me."

I recently was reminded that to get our prayers answered we are told to PRAY TO THE FATHER IN JESUS' NAME! I wonder if we all know that...and, always pray that way.

Please remind us Father, in Jesus' name. Amen

MORE OF TEXAS

While Bob was stationed at Camp Swift, TX during WWII, we rented a lovely 2nd floor room in a beautiful old Southern Colonial mansion in Austin. We were fascinated by the dense growth of stately bamboo trees next to the long driveway. We watched an army of squirrels chasing each other up & down, while a zillion butterflies fluttered about like snowflakes in Michigan.

Because we came from Detroit, we thoroughly soaked up all the amazing beauty of the palm trees, & every tropical flower. We were told the lovely Colorado River flowed nearby, & was worth using Bob's rare day off to visit.

The man at the boat docks was surprised that we wanted to rent a row boat, as most locals only use the boats in the summer. He had not rented any boats in a coupla' months, but...no reason not to, the weather was sunny & calm. He advised us where to go & where not to go.

We listened & obeyed. The scenery was truly beautiful. After about an hour, we headed back, but...all of a sudden, the wind came up, clouds gathered in minutes & we were shocked by the fierce rain.

The wind grew stronger, the oar lock broke & an oar fell overboard.

As the wind & waves increased, Bob tried frantically to alternate that one oar to prevent the boat from going in circles.

He stopped altogether & said, "Father, we know that we belong to You. You alone can bring this boat & us, safely to shore...to the right place of safety. I don't know how You will do it, but I thank You in advance. Thank you for keeping us safe & calm, in Jesus' mighty name. Amen."

I knew about Jesus, but I had not ever met Him personally, nor did I understand that kind of a prayer. My prayers had all been read from a book, & weren't really very sincere. This was a whole new experience. It was frightening, & at that moment, I almost felt numb with fear.

BUT...also at that moment, we heard a sound above the roar of the water, rain & wind. It was a voice calling, "Hello there...Hello there!" and then repeated again & again. An old man, in an old boat, pulled up beside us, threw us a rope, & towed us back to the dock. No one at the dock knew the man, nor had ever seen him before.

Thank You, Lord. Bob recently remembered that day, & laughingly said, "Yes, we truly do thank God for His wisdom & His timing...but, I've always wondered what the Colorado River is doing in Austin, Texas, anyway."

We've always wondered if it was an angel that saved us from drowning in 1940 at Lake Orion, MI...and...could it possibly have been an angel on the Colorado River in Texas? We will never know...But, we thank God, cuz we don't know how, but He did it again!

MORE MOVES

The brilliant simplicity of Alexander Graham Bell's original telephone was both exciting & functional, but I'm sure he never dreamed how it would change our lives....and move us, more ways than we expect.

In September 1940 I applied for my first real job. The earlier part-time jobs in a supermarket and a dressmaking shop were merely preparation for the stress, training and excitement ahead. One morning, from a bus window, I saw a sign in front of Michigan Bell Telephone Company, near downtown Detroit that said "Applications accepted today." I became number sixty-five in a line of one hundred three applicants for only four jobs. It was tempting to just "skip it" and go home, but the man in charge kept saying, "There's always hope...don't give up." So I didn't. My test score was 93, but others next to me had 96 and 98. It was obviously hopeless. Dismal ride home.

An 8 a.m. telephone call told me I was one of the four hired! The verbal test had been the deciding factor. Because I had lived my entire seventeen years with a Mother who was very deaf, I learned it is far wiser to enunciate, not drop your voice at the end of each sentence, & not speak loud or fast, just clearly. So my natural telephone voice was easier to hear and understand. Who could have dreamed that there was a hidden blessing related to deafness? What a shock!

In such a big busy office, everyone was given lotsa' training for every job. I was trained for five weeks to become an operator, then five more weeks for each new step up the ladder...senior operator, junior supervisor, supervisor, tandem & toll operator, & finally five more weeks to become Assistant Chief Operator in charge of all complaints. Questionable honor...but, that training has been helpful ever since.

Every new employee was issued a very long hat pin with a very large colorful knob on the end, so we could pull it quickly from our coat lapel for protection, if needed, in the neighborhood known for trouble. I chose to arrive at work at 4:30 p.m. everyday, so a taxi cab could take me home at midnight, instead of the two buses and a street car, on an earlier shift.

Two years of hard work made my job secure, but, Pearl Harbor changed everything.

Many employees chose to move to munitions plants & factories, to make guns & jeeps, and increased their salaries. But rumors said, when the war ended (SOON?) those jobs would be gone, so I stayed at Michigan Bell. My salary was 33¢ an hour, but was raised accordingly to 45¢ an hour. Hard to imagine. My weekly pay was far less than hourly pay today. But thread was 5¢ a spool & gasoline was 10¢ a gallon.

After we were married, I was given a two month leave-of-absence to visit Bob in Texas till his unit went over-seas. We were grateful that Bob stayed in Texas, when his unit shipped out & that resulted in his many moves, all over the state.

The army had moved Bob, to different camps, as I moved to nearby small towns & cities.

After the first 12 moves, my leave of absence from Michigan Bell was changed to a transfer to Southwestern Bell, which allowed me to work any place that needed me, & Bob never went overseas.

The next tiny town, not far from the Gulf of Mexico, did need my help, and I was very glad to learn that the manager could give me a ride to the telephone company office. He lived in a big house in the same town where our tacky little apartment was. His name was Ted. Everyday Ted drove me to get to work at 8 a.m. & we left there at 5 p.m.. The 20 mile ride was boring, as Ted rarely spoke & was usually grumpy.

Ted seemed to own the town. Don't most small towns have one person who "owns" everything & everybody, & seems to "run" things? Southwestern Bell owned the telephone office, but folks treated Ted like "THE BOSS."

The area seemed like wilderness, compared to the traffic & fury of Detroit. 180 degrees of sky, no traffic lights anywhere, & not even a bump that could be called a hill. Quite a change for this big city girl.

But, I had never received any training for the next challenge. The biggest change of all became clear, when I entered the telephone office for the first time. It was a tiny building that looked like a house. The large front room was empty, except for two chairs in front of a small switchboard, (commonly called a PBX board) a waste basket & a big clock.

The second seat was never used, & I became THE operator. When I needed a break, the customers just waited till I returned to take their call & ask, "Number please?"

There were no Burger King's or Wendy's anywhere. The tiny kitchen, had a two burner electric plate, but I couldn't leave the switchboard long enough to even heat soup. Sandwiches got boring. But the switchboard was busy, & kept me "hopping" to care for several small towns.

Bob's responsibilities kept him nailed to the army camp. He only left it every other night at 6 p.m., & arrived home about 6:30. I got there about 5:30 & tried to prepare meals.

When an army buddy asked Bob if I was a good cook, Bob said very seriously, "She treats me like a Greek god; she puts burnt offerings before me!"

In most small towns, the telephone operator wore many hats. "Where's the sheriff?" or "Where's the doctor?" even "Where's my Dad?" were the most common questions, requiring quick responses. Once I spent long hours playing detective. A local family had lost track of a beloved relative. How rewarding, after three days, searching all over the United States and Canada, to help reunite that family. Mr. Bell could not have foreseen the joy his phones brought them.

One day, on our ride home after work, Ted seemed unusually warm & friendly. I assumed he must be having a good day at his office. As he joked & laughed (that was a FIRST) he reached over & grabbed my leg above the knee. I froze...from SHOCK!

As I instantly removed his hand, he pulled the car over to the side of the road & turned off the engine. Totally unprepared, I grabbed for the door handle. It was locked. As I fumbled & finally unlocked the door, I frantically wondered, what do I do now? There's never any traffic on this lonely side road. Fifteen miles is a long walk. How can I get rid of him?

Ted got out on his side of the car, & headed across the front toward me. At that moment, I heard the squeal of brakes & looked over to see Bob in an Army Jeep, grinning.

He briefly assumed car trouble & asked Ted if he could help. Ted refused & said, "Thanx anyway!" As he lifted the hood, I ran, & jumped up onto the Jeep (Which was against the law...civilians must never ride in army vehicles).

I never learned why Bob was on that road that day, and an hour early. I did not tell him the whole story till after we moved again.

The next day, I resigned from that job, & Bob got orders to move to a city this time.

We finally ended up in Austin, Texas. At the local Southwestern Bell Telephone Co. office, I asked if they needed part time help. The Chief Operator was delighted to hear I had some training. It was awkward. I didn't want to lie, nor to brag. When she offered me a Supervisor's job, I asked how her employees of twenty years would accept me at my age of nineteen. She reluctantly seated me as an operator, with a Yankee accent. Now 45¢ an hour.

The courteous young operator next to me, with her sweet-talking voice, was losing all the needed circuits to the speedy Yankee operators. They, like I, had been trained to say "N'York 9:02" or "Detroit 9:02" and instantly plug in to the precious circuits, stealing all of them, while the gracious Texas girls saying, "This is Austin Texas, & my filing time is 9:01", were bewildered & frustrated. The uncompleted long distance calls were stacked two inches high & growing higher by the hour. After all, Austin was the state capital and they needed to call "out of town."

"May I help to complete some of those calls?" I asked at lunch time. "Why do you suppose I seated you there?" the chief operator asked, grinning. By 4:30 we completed the last call. No coffee breaks that day.

The next few days, several people called to express, "Thanks to the li'l Yankee operator who got my calls through." All that training paid off. The biggest surprise came in the form of a red rose and hand written thank you note from Frank Sinatra, and a typed note with a box of chocolate candy from Senator John Connelly (or was he a

26

Representative at that time?) If I had guessed that they would both become famous, I would've kept those cards. Who knew?

When World War II ended, the army moved Bob back to Detroit... the best move of all.

THE CHAPLAIN KNEW...I KNEW ABOUT

As I grew up, I was taught to be a good girl so I could, --no, so I would, go to Heaven. The bible stories about Jesus were sorta' interesting, but after awhile they weren't new anymore, & I lost interest.

The Old Testament stories were not for me. Too many people, with names I couldn't pronounce, killed too many other folks, with the same unpronounceable names. I really hated to read them, & didn't hesitate to say so, if I were asked. To be morally clean was OK, but the Bible, ...nope.

In the churches I attended as a child & teenager, we were not encouraged to read the Bible, so I didn't. I wondered if my friends did. Most teens don't discuss such things.

I had lotsa' friends from lotsa' different backgrounds. When I asked a few questions, they invited me to join them. My Jewish friends, Miriam Cooper & Paul Gold, each took me to their synagogues. They tried to answer my questions. Another friend, Bill, took me to his Christian Science meeting. He really could not answer my questions.

Then, a Lutheran girl friend, named Hazel, started asking me questions about what I believed. I went blank. I did not know what I believed about anything. So, I decided to literally go "church shopping." Methodist, Presbyterian, & Episcopalian churches were interesting.

When I started dating Bob I was seventeen & he was nineteen, both just out of high school. He talked about Jesus & praised my curiosity. He took me to the Roman Catholic "Shrine of the Little Flower" near Detroit & asked questions. We visited "Kirk of the Hills" Presbyterian Church near Detroit. We went to Nardin Park Methodist, & several others...& we just kept asking. Some of the questions were about the Bible, & how they translated the words of Jesus into action.

The priests, rabbis, ministers & leaders in each place must've been glad to see us leave. But, we still had unanswered questions. Bob said, "Maybe we're seeking a perfect church. I've heard that if we do find one, & join it, that would make it imperfect." His attempt at humor fell flat.

Bob would never tell me what church he belonged to; he didn't want me to be influenced by his choices. No need to worry, I was far too confused to consider choices.

After Pearl Harbor, Bob was drafted into the Army. On his first leave of absence as a Lieutenant, we were married in a bride's tiny chapel of Metropolitan Methodist Church in Detroit.

When I joined Bob in Texas, we attended a different church each Sunday. The small town churches were warm & friendly, but we kept looking.

At the Prisoner of War Camp, I was the only wife who lived nearby. The other wives came from great distances for brief visits, but the men all ended up at our tacky little apartment every week for cards, for cook-outs, & also for gab-fests, around our big round kitchen table.

The friendly, happy Roman Catholic Sergeant, the self-assured, dignified Episcopalian Captain, the two loud talking, arrogant Atheists, the opinionated Presbyterian Major, & one quiet Baptist Sergeant, plus Bob, the Lt. who didn't tell anyone his church preference....and then there was a Lutheran Chaplain, Arnas K. Holmio, from Michigan's Upper Peninsula.

I made sandwiches, soup, cake, cookies, coffee, lemonade & whatever else they asked for. They supplied their own root beer, coke, & ice cream. Every Wednesday they arrived promptly at 5:15 & didn't leave till 10 or 11 (or later).

After supper & card games, the men got into heated discussions & dumb conversations about politics and/or army procedures. But, somehow, as I cleared the table & did the dishes, the conversation always shifted into discussions of the Bible, & related topics. Often animated & not always courteous, they all expressed opinions & viewpoints...some founded on facts & Bible truths...much on conjecture & prejudices.

I didn't enter into the conversations, but I surely enjoyed the controversery & learned a lot. Once in a while I did ask a question & loved to "watch the fur fly", as they argued & added their opinions. To the Captain who claimed he believed some of the Bible but not all of it I asked, "How do you decide which is true?"

Somehow, there grew a strong feeling of admiration & respect for the Chaplain's quiet, calm & wise assurances of those questions & answers. Over the many weeks, the two handsome Atheists stopped being quite so determined. The other men all developed a more serious, less judgmental attitude toward the comments made & questions asked.

One evening, Chaplain Holmio told us he was leaving to visit other

28

Prisoner of War side camps. That was his final visit for awhile. One of the men asked him point blank, "So, tell us Chaplain, after all the jibber-jabber, what have we learned? Sum it up briefly for us, please?"

Calmly, serenely, with deeply convincing tone of voice, he slowly started, "Well, you fellas are all a bunch of Ecumaniacs who seem to have your own opinions...nothing wrong with that I guess, but, if I have strong trust in a bridge & it collapses in a storm, what good is my trust? And ...if there's a big platter of fried chicken on the table, it does me no good, no matter how it looks & smells, unless I take it & make it my own. I'm not sure that makes sense to y'all so, let's cut the nonsense & mention a few facts that I trust—and—have made my own. It's up to each of you, what you'll do with them.

First, both the Old & New Testaments echo the same basic facts. God loves us so much He sent His only Son, Jesus, to die to take the punishment & power of sin from our lives (if we let Him).

So, if we accept Jesus as our OWN Savior & make Him the Lord of our lives, we have become a Christian. That doesn't eliminate problems, it means He will help us through them & forgive us when we goof off... (& we all do) ...when we ask Him. Folks ask which church is the right one. Really, those of us who call Jesus our Savior ARE the church, and whichever building we worship in, is secondary. Whoever believes that the Bible is the true WORD of God, written by people who were inspired by the Holy Spirit; if they treat others with love & respect; if they're generous (with what God gives them) both to Him & to others in need,... well then, it doesn't matter what the name is over the church door. OK? I guess that sez it, so G'nite, & God bless y'all in the name of Jesus Christ. Praise Him & love each other!" He clicked his heels together, sharply saluted, & burst out the door, with tears streaming down his face. The other men wiped their eyes, acting sorta' flustered. I guess men have more trouble admitting their emotions than women do. I wiped my tears on the dish towel.

The seven men seemed a bit more courteous, less rowdy, and more serious, as the evening ended. I wondered if I was the only one who heard answers that evening to questions I'd been searching for all my life.

I had been trying to get Jesus to love me, and then I learned that He already did, and, I only needed to thank Him, & act like I meant it, by the way I treated others, and praised Him. I needed to accept Him publicly; which I did the next Sunday in a tiny little Baptist church in Bastrop, Texas.

After learning that the Bible really is God's Word, I developed a desire to read it. I learned that being good to earn "Brownie Points" cannot get me to Heaven. HE DID IT, and so I wanted to be good, in gratitude!

Many years, later I located the Chaplain as the Dean of a Lutheran College in Northern Michigan, & I wrote to him. I thanked him for letting God use him to bring us to Jesus. I told him that many Pastors & Preachers told us how to act like Christians, but when he told me how to BECOME a Christian, I did. It was great to tell him that Bob & I had a Christian home, & we wanted him to know it. His letter in return told of his tears of joy & gratitude to God & to me for writing. That was in October. The Christmas card I sent him in December was returned by his family. He had died. I'm so glad I wrote when I did.

Chaplain Homio had a few sayings & ideas that he shared:

1. God catches His fish before He cleans them. We try to clean folks up & bring them to Jesus. We need to get out of the way & let HIM do it.
2. God doesn't create winners or losers. He creates choosers.
3. God doesn't love us more because we are good. He always loves us because HE is good.
4. We cannot do anything to make God love us more, nor can we do anything to make God love us less. When we Praise Him it pleases Him. When we sin, it hurts us & makes Him sad.
5. Whining, complaining & worrying are insults to God...& they sure don't do us any good, anyway.
6. To know about Jesus isn't enough. We must get to know Jesus. His Word helps us to do that. The Bible is His love letter to us.
7. When we pray, we must not ask Jesus to be with us, as so many folks do. He promised in Matthew 28:20 "and lo, I am with you always, even unto the end of the world. Amen." If we ask Him to be with us, it's an insult...as tho' we don't believe Him. Instead, let's ask Him to help us KNOW (or be aware) of His presence. And Chaplain Holmio always added, "Thank God, He MEANT it!"
8. God also tells us that His Word..."*shall not return...void.*" Isaiah 55:11 so, let's remember and believe that too!

Bob & I often thanked God for the precious experiences we had with Chaplain Holmio, & all that we learned from him.

SMILES

There isn't much humor in most election campaigns. As one young candidate moved from one handshake to the next at a local retirement home, his smile had begun to look "glued-on", certainly less than sincere.

He repeated his name over & over to each potential voter. "I'm Joe Blow, & I hope you plan to vote for me."

One little lady sat in her wheelchair, quietly watching from the door of her apartment. As the activity subsided, the candidate spotted her. He rushed over, leaned down to shake her hand with both of his, saying, "Do you know my name, dear?"

"No, but if you stop over at that desk, that nice lady will tell you," she answered with a real smile.

––––––––––

Have you heard about the man driving thru L.A. with three penguins in his backseat? A policeman stopped him, & warned him, "If you don't take those penguins to Sea World I'll have to arrest you!"

"Yes sir, I certainly will." he answered.

The next day, same time, same place, same car, same three penguins. The policeman was very annoyed. "I thought I made it clear, and you promised to take those penguins to Sea World. What happened?"

The man answered, "Yes sir, I sure did...& we had such a good time, that today I'm taking them to Disneyland!"

––––––––––

We can agree that PRO and CON are opposites. Do we also agree that progress is the opposite of Congress?

IS IT WONDERFUL?

Webster defines WONDER as a cause of surprise & astonishment, amazement, strange admiration, a miracle.

FULL doesn't mean partial nor half full. It means "to the top"...to the very top.

When I hear someone say, "That's a wonderful toy"...or..."What a wonderful lunch we had," etc., I'm usually cynical, a bit annoyed or sometimes it's even disgusting. I hope I remember not to say those things.

How can a lunch excite marvelous extra ordinary astonishment? Can a toy be so unique, so amazingly curious, as to be called wonderful? Can new drapes or a new paint job on the wall ever be categorized as a miraculous event? Perhaps to some folks. And some folks may disagree....

But...I prefer to save that gloriously amazing word to describe the rarely seen array of deep luminous colors, changed into the lightest, palest beauty in a sunset or a rainbow, or gorgeous fall colors. Maybe a tiny infant's first smile or first step or first word, could fit perfectly. Or, how about the joy of knowing that a beloved child was not injured in a terrible auto accident? Now that is truly wonderful!

The magic of love shared between husband & wife, or parents & children, or friends, regardless of age or race or title, can certainly qualify as wonderful. The bulbs planted in the fall, endured the rain & freezing cold, & now have glorious blooms...that's wonderful!

Those are tiny examples of the wonder that God fills our lives with, constantly. God's love that sent Jesus to die to take the punishment & power of sin from our lives & then ROSE again, is the most wonderful of all. The love we learn from HIM, permeates our lives, our families, & inspires us to share HIS love with those around us. That helps others to define & enjoy the true meaning of WONDERFUL!

I WONDER (A WONDER-FULL LIST)

Another definition of WONDER might be: I wish I knew.

For many years I found the syndicated column written by Sidney Harris a source of fascination. He never seemed to run out of "Things I've Learned On The Way To Looking Up Something Else." Perhaps if he had lived longer he might have found answers to some of the questions that leap-frog through my mind. Here a few that make me wonder.

- Why does the car ahead of me stay so far back that only he can turn left when the light changes?
- Why do children grow so fast the month after they all get new clothes?
- Why are the best movies on T.V. when it is time to turn it off to go to bed?
- Why do the hurry-up meals so often turn out better than the ones I

spend all day preparing?

- Why do I forget what I want to buy in the store...until I get home and plan to use it?
- Why does my sewing machine bobbin thread run out when I'm in a hurry and have two inches left to sew?
- Why isn't the shade of thread I need available, when there are millions of them in the stores?
- Why do kids love to play in a sink filled with water, till we put dirty dishes in it?
- Why do things go on sale the week after I buy them?
- Why do I always sit behind the tall person and in front of the one whose foot taps on my chair?
- Why does the cash register tape run out in the line I'm in?
- Why wouldn't it be fun and exciting to see the sun come up in the west and go down in the east?
- Why do some small, simple objects cost so much, and some complex, more expensive looking things cost so little?
- Why do movies of horse-drawn wagons look like the wheels rotate backwards? Someone told me, but I can't remember.
- Why do fair skinned folks seek a suntan, but some dark skinned folks use creams and stuff to lighten their skin tones?
- Why do people delight in tickling those who are ticklish?
- Why do newspaper and T.V. decision makers assume everyone loves sports?
- Why don't the colors of flowers and grass fade in the sun? Our clothing usually does. Even drapes & rugs fade in the sun.
- Why do politicians insult us by using the same old lies and ploys that have failed for years? For decades? For centuries?
- Why do so many folks believe those lies, again & again & again to even re-elect the wrong person?
- Why don't birds get discouraged when it takes so long to fly back home?
- Why does God surround us with gorgeous green grass and trees, blue skies and flowers in riotous shades and shapes, when we humans do such damaging things to our world?
- Why do so many people chew with their mouths open when it is sooo rude and unappetizing? Could it be because their parents do?
- Why do so few people look in a full length mirror to see how they really look?
- Why, when it is so gratifying to hear children say "please" and "thank you", do so few parents teach them to do so?

33

- Why do so few parents treat their children with respect to set the example? Why do so many children turn out good in spite of their parents?
- Why does that last wee scrap of soap stick to the sink (& everything else) except to the new bar where I want it to stick?
- Why do things I drop always jump under the stove or the refrigerator & hide somewhere?
- Why does that fly buzzing around my lamp shade in January think it's June?
- When cars straddle the lines in a crowded parking lot, does that mean the drivers are selfish or stupid? Do they ever feel guilty?
- Why can't I remember someone or something till the middle of the night?
- Why do all the cars in the county drive by just as I cross the road to my mailbox—& where do they all go when I get back to my door?
- Where is that other sock?
- Why do my windshield wipers work so hard they squeak when it drizzles—but quit when it rains hard?
- When I watch a late movie, why do I fall asleep the last 5 minutes before I learn WHO DUNNIT?
- Why do the items I prefer (& those I've learned to love) get discontinued?
- Where are the policemen when the "crazies" zoom in & out of traffic & run thru red lights?
- Why do pages stick together?
- Why do newspapers & T.V. saturate us with the same stuff, but conceal the facts we're seeking?
- Why does that same song stick in my head all day, even if I hate it?
- When I add a column of figures, why do I get a different answer every time? Don't answer that!
- Why are there coupons for all the items I never buy?
- Who stays up all nite to hide that tiny end of thread on the new spool?
- Why do folks criticize teen drivers when many reports show its older drivers who cause many of the problems?
- Why don't folks look in a mirror, instead of just assuming things look good—because they're "in style?"
- Am I the only one who's sick of looking at jeans?
- Why does the Lord Jesus Christ continue to love us when we are soooo unlovable?
- Where do the cleansing tissues hide when I know I empty ALL the

34

pockets before putting things in the washer?
- Why do folks with REAL problems rarely complain, while those who do complain often have few problems?
- When you pull that little thread why does the button fall off?
- Why does that fone call I've been waiting for, come just at the crucial moment on the T.V. show I've watched for 1 hr & 50 minutes?
- If bathtubs became available in about 1850 & telephones were invented about 1875, why wasn't I born then, so I could sit in my tub for an hour without the fone ringing?
- How do butterflies know how to weave that amazing little cocoon, when & how to come out, & who chooses their gorgeous colors?
- If that balloon was full of air & floating high last night, why did it fall sadly on the floor this morning? Who steals the air? How?
- Why is it so difficult to locate reliable shops and reliable people to repair clocks, lamps, et cetera? Is it cuz so many folks throw it away if it's broken? (Even broken people...often get thrown away).
- Why is the joy of a "JOB WELL DONE" still more gratifying than "GET THE JOB DONE?"
- Why do so many things look good on the menu, and I get full so fast?
- Why are we surprised at the creativity, brilliance and good manners of children, especially our children?
- Why was it so great to have a gentleman open the door and smile graciously when I said, "Chivalry isn't dead." He then reminded me, "It takes a lady to prompt a gentleman to be chivalrous." Wouldn't that please you too?

Some questions have obvious answers; some have no answers. And... I wonder...no, I suspect that most of us wouldn't know where to search for them. Whatever would I look up, in order to find these things on the way to learn them? Oh, well! I didn't really need to know anyway. Why am I asking?

IT REALLY DID HAPPEN ONE NIGHT

I clearly remember the siren sounds of the fast approaching ambulance and police cars, the blinding lights of oncoming vehicles and the screams of little Linda, after that terrible crash.

We had spent a wonderful day in San Diego, visiting Bob's sister, & her family. About 7 p.m. we left for the three hour drive to Whittier, with my sister & her daughter, Beverly, who was driving.

Beverly was used to driving in Los Angeles traffic, and her quick reflexes probably saved our lives, when the big car from Texas ran the red light & hit us broadside. Two other cars stopped, & folks from Kansas & Colorado told the officers the accident was not our fault. Even though that happened in 1966, I can still smell the heavy odors of hot metal, spilled gasoline & blood, in the California hot night air.

Ambulances & police cars surrounded us. Sirens were screaming, & brakes squealed, as cars careened around to avoid a big pile up, in the fast moving traffic, near Escondido.

The car that hit us had left Disneyland one hour earlier, & that was nearly 70 miles away. They weren't hurt, but were taken away by police.

As the rest of us sat, wondering what to do, Ron stumbled out of the back seat, limped in pain, over to a curb, & sat dazed, as more police cars arrived. Sixteen year old boys often feel undefeatable, so it came as a shock to him to stagger & feel faint. He was stunned to see his Dad & his Aunt Helen. They were both bleeding so profusely that an entire box of cleansing tissues turned red instantly in Bob's hands.

The new white "Mary Poppins" pinafore, that seven year old Linda was so proud of, was now totally red. Linda clung to me, sobbing quietly.

Our small rented car had only four seat belts for six passengers. Neither my sister, Helen seated center front, nor I seated center back, had seat belts. So I was thrust forward, pushing her into the windshield, at point of impact. Bob seated in the front passenger's seat was thrust into the dashboard!

The ambulance crew & several policemen kept reassuring us all, "You guys sure are lucky to have your seatbelts on! Your husband would have been decapitated for sure!" We didn't feel or look lucky.

Helen's injuries were very serious. The ambulance crew worked immediately & efficiently on her, & on Bob, to stop the bleeding. Then they shoved Bob's stretcher into the lower left, like a huge "drawer" of the ambulance. Helen was placed in the lower right "drawer" & Linda's stretcher was threaded gently into place, hanging directly over her beloved Daddy. She patted his arm as they moved her up & over him.

Beverly, Ron, & I crowded into the front seat for the three block screeching trip to the hospital. At the emergency room entrance, the ambulance was parked with the open end close to a wide open door. The staff swiftly took Helen & Bob in, & started their procedures.

While they were being cared for so quickly, I glanced out & saw Linda's tiny feet on that high shelf of the ambulance. I went out & reached up to pat those little feet, certain that our wee seven year old girl must be puzzled & frightened, being strapped firmly into place in that dark space.

She'd been hearing strange sounds & unfamiliar voices. So, in my most calm & comforting tone, I tried to assure her, "Hi, Honey girl, Mommy & Daddy are just inside. The nurses will be out to get you down very soon, so don't be afraid, OK?"

"Oh, Mommy, I'm not afraid. I've just been talking to God & asking Him to make Daddy & Aunt Helen brave...& make the doctor smart! And He will!"

Oh, dear Lord, give me that kind of pure faith, I whispered silently, as I kissed her tiny feet. My eyeglasses were missing, so I was cautious getting back into the building.

A rather amusing thing we learned later, ALL of our glasses, & purses, & ALL our shoes ended up under the dashboard. Obviously, they were not nailed down, & all flew forward. Strange.

Nurses & interns applied a wee bandage to Bev's chin, & an Ace bandage to Ron's sprained ankle. They took Linda, lovingly, for X-rays. Black & blue marks from the seatbelt worsened, but we rejoiced that she had no serious injuries. My shins & thumbs hurt, but were not broken.

As they worked on Helen, they kept asking her, her name. Later, she told us how annoyed she was that they didn't write it down, not realizing that they were testing her, to know the extent of her injuries. Having been thrust into the windshield, it then took 50 minutes for two nurses & an intern to remove the glass shards from her forehead. Her eyebrow had been severed & shoved above her forehead, & was on the top of her head. Her collarbone had punctured her lung. Now that was serious!

A young doctor came to tell us that Bob & Helen were to be admitted to the hospital. No surprise, of course. A nurse suggested I may want to kiss him "G'nite" before she rolled him away on the gurney.

"He's completely covered with blood. I can't find a place to kiss," was my feeble attempt to sound nonchalant, as I kissed him.

"Hey, just like Clark Gable after a fight scene!" was my Bob's quick response, as they wheeled him down the hall. We did not yet know that under all the bandages, his eye was forced below its socket, his cheek bone was broken in several places, & his teeth were jarred out of place. But, in all that pain & trauma, he found humor.

After the nurses more fully examined Linda, they gently wrapped her in a big blue flannel blanket, hugging & consoling her. They stuffed the blood soaked sweater, pinafore & sox into a plastic tote bag. She looked so tiny on that big stretcher in the hectic, busy, starkly cold room.

Bev, Ron & I sat on a long hard bench watching Linda eat animal crackers.

"It's hard to eat lying down, Mommy," she said. She had no idea what was ahead. Neither did we.

Our biggest challenge was what to do next. The car was a pile of debris. Our belongings, broken glasses, broken shoes & sandals, & bloody sweaters, were all mashed into plastic tote bags on the floor beside the bench. We were 80 miles from Helen's & Bev's home in Whittier & 2,500 miles from ours in Saginaw, MI. Where & how do you find a place to sleep near a downtown hospital at 11 p.m. in a strange city?

From out of nowhere, I seemed to hear "Be still and know that I am God!" I took a deep breath & felt more able to face the next problem.

Ron limped to a nearby desk & asked an employee for the numbers of the police department & the local newspaper. At that time of night who else would be open? After giving a brief but vivid description of our situation, Ron asked for suggestions. The newspaper employees supplied the name & number of a downtown hotel, above some stores & a bar. Recently purchased by new owners, "It's now respectable," came the odd information, intended to reassure us. The police cautioned us to "lock all doors & be very careful." They then offered to take us there.

Ron's initiative & TAKE CHARGE attitude warmed this Mother's heart. In a very official tone, he asked, "May we please borrow this blanket to keep my sister warm? You know we'll be back & return it as soon as we wash the blood from her clothes." Of course, they agreed. The nurse smilingly wrapped Linda tightly & kissed her on the forehead, saying "Sleep well," as we left that cold Emergency Room, filled with warm people.

The policemen who drove us, had to slowly search for the door to that second floor hotel. It seemed hidden by all the stores & bar lights. The coffee shop & dry cleaners were obviously closed, & the bar was obviously open, blaring with lights & noise.

One of the officers carried Linda up the brightly lit stairway. A huge sign hung suspended in clear sight. Bold letters said NO DRUNKS ALLOWED. At first, the officer was speechless. Then, he checked out the owners, & helped us get settled. We had no luggage, just tote bags full of bloody clothing, broken glasses & broken shoes.

The other officer then said awkwardly & too loud, "I'm sure you'll be safe here. Call if you need anything else." We thanked both of them again & again.

We were greeted warmly by a man & his wife, who treated us like family. They made the next few days bearable ... even pleasant, at times. They instantly apologized. "That goofy driver was not from Escondido!" They then supplied us with four pairs of assorted pajamas, two electric fans, a tray of fresh sandwiches, a pitcher of frosty lemonade & a tub of soap powder to wash bloody clothing.

Ron smirked, "I didn't expect to find another Dad & Mom here."

As soon as I bathed Linda & threaded her into those big pajamas, she fell asleep. The shower felt great to remove all the dried blood, & it was sooo nice to have clean pajamas. Linda's clothes & all our underwear were washed & hung on coat hangers near the fans, to dry.

We four slept soundly in that big old room with three clean beds. No one cared that the drapes were all different lengths, the bedspreads were terrible colors, & we had no toothbrushes. Just before I dozed off I remembered, Jesus said, "I am with you always!" Thank you, Lord!

About 7 a.m. Linda's pinafore & the other things were all dry, & white again. Our outer wear was all caked with dried blood, but we, and our undies, were all clean & dry.

We couldn't get into the hospital till 9, so we headed for the coffee shop next to the now silent bar. We all felt embarrassed to wear such soiled clothes, so, when the light went on at the laundry & dry cleaners, we ran past the coffee shop, & burst into the doorway, as they unlocked the door of the dry cleaners.

An employee instantly called the manager, who brought us three large paper robes. He took all the blood soaked clothing in one arm, & with a sly grin, he handed Linda, in her white pinafore, a stack of comic books & a lollipop. About 40 minutes later, he returned with three coat hangers carrying our clean-as-new clothing. When I tried to pay him, he grabbed my hand, closing his fingers over mine, insisting, "Hey...that's the least we can do for y'all. And, little Honey, you keep a big bunch of those books. A hospital waiting room can be plenty boring for a doll like you." Linda hugged him.

Early that morning we had tried to call Helen's husband, Carl, in Whittier, but got no answer. After working the night shift, he had stopped to get the oil changed in his car. It probl'y was better that he didn't try to drive that three hours with no sleep, anyway. Better call again later.

Now we were ready for breakfast. Money was so scarce we chose to order two meals for the four of us. The waitress had seen us "fly by" earlier, so her first question was, "What's up?"

The tale was briefly retold. We praised those nice folks in the hotel upstairs & in the dry cleaners, for their kindness. We repeated our order for two breakfasts. "NO way, I can't possibly take your money...you'll each get a meal so you can get outa' here fast... and...the man next door paid for you all to eat lunch & supper here too...for FREE! You'll need all your money before this week is over!"

By that time she was popping bread in the toaster & cooking eggs & ham like she had six hands. That was one of the tastiest & quickest meals I ever ate.

It was now 9 o'clock so we hurried the three blocks to the hospital. Helen was buried in tubes, needles & bandages, but alert & glad to see us. Bob's face had turned totally black & blue. A fast walking, fast talking doctor said into the air, without facing me, "His eye was forced down into the cavity below & we don't know what to expect. We think his other eye might be OK. The bones in his cheek are broken. The pain will be intense...He will lose the one eye entirely. We're trying to save the other one."

My reply was, "I thank God he's alive!"

"Well lady, remind yourself of that often. The next few hours & days will be the most difficult time of your lives!" he announced firmly, & walked away. I was stunned. The next day he avoided me. I chased him down the halls, but he rushed in & out of rooms, pretending not to see me. He gave me no more information.

When I called the church office in Saginaw, they said we were all on the prayer chain. It was good to feel the comforting reassurance of our friends & the love of our beloved "Doctor" Jesus, on our case.

Because Bob was expected to return to his job in Saginaw, I called his "BIG BOSS" at the main office in Detroit, with all the details. Bob had been a store manager for over 18 years & it was truly gratifying to hear the owner of the entire chain of thirty stores say, "If Bob needs ANYTHING...even a specialist from Switzerland flown in...you call me

& we'll do it! Got that? Hey, how are you & the two kids doing, OK?" I said we were doing fine. Then, he burst out, "NOW, I want you to call me about noon my time, every day...COLLECT...I'll be waiting at my office every day. OK?" How reassuring.

Beverly, Ron & I now had to make some vital decisions. Bob & Helen were now considered stable. So:

1. Because Helen's husband had worked all night in Whittier & didn't even know what happened, we had to choose the best way to tell him. If we called him, he'd be shocked, but sleepy, and...insist on driving 90 miles while tired.
2. Helen & Bob had improved enough that their lives were no longer in danger. Carl's few more hours of sleep were important for his safety.
3. If Bev & Ron took a Greyhound bus they could reach Whittier before Carl awoke, so they could tell him in person; better than a phone call.
4. Bev & Ron could gather clean clothes for all of us & bring more money back, riding with Carl.

Our next challenge was to locate the bus station, the schedule, & the money for two tickets. My purse & Beverly's contained nearly enough. Ron dug deep in his pockets, & supplied a bit more. We lacked just twenty cents. Should we borrow it from those nice hotel folks?

"Mommy, dya' want my two dimes?" Linda asked wistfully, as she dug into her Disneyland purse. We all laughed out loud, & bought two bus tickets for Whittier. Bev & Ron left 25 minutes later.

At the hospital, the Grey Ladies entertained Linda with coloring books & checkers, while I visited Bob & Helen. Because Bob's eye had been forced through the floor of his eye socket, the two California eye specialists predicted his sight would never recover & he should expect constant pain for the rest of his life. Surgery might be an option, but he must either return to Michigan within a week or plan to stay in California for at least six weeks. That was the next vital decision to be made. SOON.

Later, that doctor who had avoided me, came looking for me & excitedly declared, "The most amazing thing just happened!" His puzzled expression & high pitched tone of voice caught my attention.

"Your husband's eye went back into its proper position all by ITSELF. The other eye is clear & fine. It is truly amazing!"

"Doctor, Can you believe that it was answered prayer...that God did it? There are dozens of folks in California & Michigan praying. Yes, GOD did it!" Was my quick response.

His long, pensive silence ended with, "Welllll, I've never been a praying man...but...if this is the result, I just might take it up, seriously." His head down, he hurried down the hall, as I stood crying with relief and gratitude. Sincere gratitude!

When I called Bob's boss the next day, he was genuinely concerned & kept offering to help. But the help we needed he could not supply.

What I did not mention before, was our train trip to Los Angeles & all the related circumstances.

FIRST: The employees of several airlines went on strike, thus thousands of folks tried to take trains instead of flying.

SECOND: Because Bob had been told he must be back in Michigan within a week; we must get him on one of the few emergency flights available. He did qualify, but there were hundreds ahead of him.

THIRD: Our train tickets were no longer valid because we had missed the scheduled dates, and...no new tickets were available; too many planes were down.

FOURTH: There were riots & serious tension in Chicago, where we had parked our car, near the train station. I called the parking lot staff to tell them of our accident, & we'd be delayed. We expected to pay the additional fee. As they always collected in advance, our car was on "borrowed time." There was no assurance that our car would even be there, when we returned, I was told.

At the airline ticket office, the staff & the manager were not helpful, not even courteous, as we explained to them the urgency of getting Bob on a plane & back to Saginaw within the next three days.

Every morning & every afternoon, we returned to leave another slip of paper with data, about where Bob must go, & where I could be reached, at anytime. They were so annoyed they wanted to shout at me, & order me out of the office. I assured the manager that we had prayed about it & Bob MUST be on a plane before the end of the next day! He left the room & slammed his office door each time he saw me arrive. On the morning of that final day, as I arrived, the telephone rang. There was an unexpected cancellation. The employees were shocked! It was a non-stop flight, directly to Tri-City Airport near Saginaw. The manager came out of his office grinning, & asked, "Can you make it there? The plane will leave in three hours & it takes almost an hour to reach the airport!" As we grabbed the ticket, I ran behind the counter & hugged him. That shocked everyone. But, we did get Bob on the plane.

A phone call to our Pastor & friends in Saginaw alerted them to meet his plane & drive him to our home there. It hurt me to think of Bob at

42

home alone, after that long plane ride, but, we had no options.

"Lord, we are so glad You are caring for our Dad," Ron said, as we left the airport.

Back at the hospital, Helen's shattered body was healing faster than expected. After Bev & Ron had returned with Carl in his car, it was good to have clean clothes & more money. We five moved to a motel with a bit more privacy & less noise. We thanked that gracious couple, who had been so kind to us in their funny old hotel. The next day Helen was released & we all returned to their home in Whittier.

We kept thinking of Bob, but the telephone in Saginaw did not answer no matter when we called. Was he in a hospital in Saginaw, or staying with a friend?

Now we must get new train tickets to take Ron, Linda & me back to Chicago, to claim our orphan car & drive home.

It had seemed difficult to get Bob on an airplane...but...that was simple compared to the ordeal we faced getting anyone to even TALK to us about train reservations. The airline strike had forced thousands to take trains. The long lines at Union Station in Los Angeles were daunting. After another three hour wait on the second day, we were told "Sorry...it will be 17 days before we can get three seats for you on the same train. In twelve days we can get two...next please!" They literally were moving people, bodily, out of the lines. People were crying & yelling.

BUT, Ron & Linda & I REFUSED to move over to relinquish our place in that long line. I retold THE story of our tragic accident. This was not just a vacation, this was urgent. I showed the agent our unused tickets. "There's no one to care for my injured husband. I MUST get there. They flew him emergency status. PLEEEZE help us get there!" Big pause.

We had prayed that morning that we could by-pass the red-tape to get on a train in front of all those vacationers. All of a sudden, the ticket agent slapped his hand on the counter & shouted, "Hey I just found three seats on the same train. Not in the same car though, will that work? Can you make it? They'll leave here in six hours!"

Linda was perched on tip toe beside me & listening intently. She shouted, "Oh yes mister, now we can see my Daddy. He has one eye covered up & needs me to be his "Seeing eye daughter." You're such a nice man. I'll always remember YOU!" His weary strained expression burst into a big grin. It made his day brighter.

Ron enjoyed the sense of independence it gave him to travel by himself for two days & two nights, except when he came to "help" us get to the dining car, on that long full train.

As we left the train in Chicago, Ron limped to get all our luggage. Three large suitcases & three tote bags were difficult to handle for two long blocks to the parking lot to our car. (That was before luggage had wheels.)

The parking lot attendant could have easily won a role as a cruel villain in a Hollywood movie. His facial scars, missing tooth, unruly hair hanging over & under a dirty rag around his forehead, & a scowl that would frighten a tiger...made my pulse rate increase, as he approached us.

With her head tipped to one side, Linda said, "Are you the nice man who took good care of our car? My Daddy got hurt real bad & they let him fly home all by himself. But we don't know how he is...can you find our car? Do you know where Saginaw is? My Mommy never drove there before."

The man's grim, cold expression softened as he leaned over to talk to Linda. He picked her up & she hugged him. Her long red wavy hair & stark white complexion was an interesting contrast to his very black hair & mahogany skin. He then took a crinkled envelope out of his pocket & drew a very accurate map out of Chicago, & handed it to Ron with a big grin, "Here fella, you be the navigator, OK?"

When I started to write the check for the additional two weeks, I asked what the charge would be. That wonderful ugly giant stopped my hand saying, "It wasn't your fault that y'all had an accident, I'm glad no harm came to the rest of you, & I'm glad I could keep your car safe from all that bad craziness here. You paid for the first four weeks, so that's enough...OK?" Linda hugged his big wide knees, & he got tears in his eyes. His directions were clear & easy to follow.

From California we had tried many times to call Bob, but could never reach him...it was busy or no answer every time. As we got closer on the train, our anxiety increased. From Chicago, we still had not gotten an answer...not even from our neighbor's phone in Michigan. And, of course we were sooooo eager to get home. Was he in the hospital?

The six hour drive from Chicago seemed like 16. All of the events & images of the past two weeks skipped through my mind. Linda just slept in the back seat. Ron feared I'd get sleepy at the wheel. No danger of that. I was eager.

The big shock came as we saw Bob, standing in the driveway, washing mud off the driveway with the garden hose. His Mother & her lady friend had come from Detroit on a bus to cook & care for him. He claimed that "hundreds" of folks from the church had brought cakes, & casseroles, & to check up on him. We knew it was an exaggeration till we opened the refrigerator, & then understood.

Bob had tried to call us in Whittier the day he got home. No answer. The next two days he called "everyone" in Saginaw to tell them he was home...hence...all the busy signals we kept getting. Then, for two more days, folks took him to local doctors & dentists...and...when he got home; he left the fone off the hook to get some sleep. When he called us in California, we were at the train depot, while Helen was at the doctor's office. It became comical,...later...much later.

Ron's sprained ankle, the stitches on Bev's face, Linda's many bruises & my injured thumbs & shins, all healed quickly. It took many months for Helen's rib, her collar bone, & the scars on her face & neck to heal. The insurance company resisted, but finally paid.

For the next few weeks, Bob stopped regularly in the offices of the dentist, the oral surgeon & the ophthalmologist. Each report was improvement. We were told that the eye area is so small & so perfectly formed, there is no extra space to accommodate scar tissue that forms after all serious injuries. The pain will be permanent. Obviously God had other plans. Soon the pain disappeared completely & Bob had 20/20 vision within six months...in BOTH eyes! The doctors were all amazed & we are still thanking the Lord!!!

By October I found time to write sincere thank you notes to the parking lot attendants in Chicago, & to all those folks in Escondido. I couldn't locate addresses & names for all of them, so I wrote one letter to the Escondido newspaper, telling them the whole amazingly horrible & wonderful story. It was a long story with dozens of leading characters. The newspaper employees, the policemen, the ambulance crew, the emergency room & other hospital staff, the doctors, the Grey Ladies, the hotel owners, the dry cleaners, the coffee shop, the airline ticket office, the train station agent, (have I skipped anyone?) well, we wanted them all to know how they blessed us.

At Christmas, we received a big fat heavy envelope from the hotel owners. In it, was a newspaper (dated the day after our accident), with a picture of us on the highway getting into the ambulance (Bob's sister had seen it the next day & nearly fainted). The second newspaper was the (Oct. issue) "Second Front Page." Across the top was a copy of the letter I had sent to them in October, listing & thanking all those who had been so kind, so helpful, & so gracious to us. It was greatly enlarged, exactly as I wrote it...and...below it the editor had added:

"We hear far too many sad stories with sad endings. We feel this happy ending needs to be enlarged & spread around. The deep gratitude is real. Read it. Read it again. Read it again...and then do those good deeds over & over again. Good job, Escondido!"

We constantly repeat, "Thank You, Lord, You did it again!"

———————

LINDA'S NAP

When Linda was about 18 months old, she was safely strapped into the car seat, playing with her dolly, and dozed off to sleep. I had to drop off a sweater at a friend's house. I hated to disturb Linda's sweet nap, so I parked in my friend's driveway, turned off the engine, removed the key, slipped quietly out without slamming the door, and ran the 19 feet up to hand the sweater to my friend on her porch.

In that few seconds, Linda had awakened and sleepily grabbed for those interesting things that stuck out from "Mommy's Wheel". Many times I had reminded her "don't touch Mommy's wheel."

Maybe that's why the newer infant car seats fit in the back seats. Anyway, Linda was groggy and had no idea that she had shoved the gear into neutral, allowing the car to slide slowly, very slowly, down the slightly slanted driveway. In those few seconds, as the car began to move backwards, I screamed in panic, "Oh no, Lord! Oh no! Oh no, Lord!"

There was no way I could grab the door or the fender. I just kept screaming. I'm not sure why I screamed "NO!", but I truly do know why I screamed, "Oh Lord!". He was the only one who COULD help.

The car very slowly slid to the end of the slanted driveway and across the street, into the neighbor's flat driveway and came to a total stop. As I opened the car door, Linda's wide grin assured me she was okay. Of course, my reaction was, "Thank you, Lord. You did it again!"

P.S. Later, we measured it, and agreed that even 19 feet was too far to leave a baby alone!

KIDS...KIDS...KIDS

I've heard it said, "Don't talk about your kids...for two good reasons:
1. Folks have kids of their own & are not interested in yours...or
2. Folks do not have kids & are not interested in yours." WELL, I'm taking a chance that you may be interested anyway. In case you are not...Sorry, I repent.

1946

Nadene, our first baby, learned to talk when she was a week old, or so it seemed. When she was about 18 months old (or close to that...after all it was 1946) we remember her "jibber-jabbering like a magpie." It was fun trying to translate.

When she saw me put lipstick on, she begged, "Stiplick on Dene?" When she wanted spaghetti & cottage cheese, she asked for "baasketti" & "kaaa sheese." Bob's umbrella caused her to giggle & ask, "numberella, Daddy?" & he would open & close it again & again & again as she danced & clapped her hands. "Hope she's always so easy to please," Bob grinned.

It took us awhile to learn that "brow-eyes" & "carmonony" meant eyebrows & macaroni. We didn't want to laugh & make a fuss about her (basswords) backward words. We weren't sure if it would have any effect on her future speech. But, after her bath, when she kept saying, "Bowder baby donson," it took us a moment to catch on. As she pointed, we "got it" & we both enjoyed using Johnson Baby Powder all over li'l dimpled dolly, & agreed that was really funny.

She laughed & clapped whenever she saw "flutterbies" in the yard & was never afraid of what she called "bitedogs."

One morning, Nadene became restless in her highchair before we finished eating, so I washed off the tray to offer her some toys. We certainly couldn't put her down on the floor till I had my jogging shoes on to chase her. As I wiped the tray with a wash cloth, she tried to take it from my hands. So, I got a clean cloth & let her wash her own tray. She heard someone call it a washrag & that became her theme song from then on. It seemed like every hour (or every five minutes) all day long, she kept saying (no, it became more like insisting) "Shrag"..."Shrag!" It took a constant supply of clean wash cloths, & our house was never cleaner. I decided a clean damp cloth wouldn't hurt any of our furniture.

Nadene pitty-patted all over, all day & I was glad she found a harmless hobby at such a young age. But, one day she wiped Bob's face, as he lay sleeping on the sofa after mowing. She kept smiling & telling him, "Shrag Daddy." We all giggled. Bob lifted her high in the air & proclaimed, "Baby doll, we're gonna find you another hobby!"

1947

I've never ever seen anything cuter than our wee two year old looking out the window at the morning fog. Both of her chubby hands under that dimpled chin...and she said, in a woeful voice, "What a froggy day...Mama, where are the frogs?"

1949

Four year old Nadene was holding tightly to the tall vertical pole behind the bus driver, as her mother attempted to put coins in the big receptacle beside him. Too many packages, too many people in the way, too much movement, as the bus lurched to & fro.

The bus driver barked, "Hurry up there lady...you're blocking traffic!"

The coins dropped in, & her mother took Nadene's hand to rush to a seat, but her other hand held tightly to that pole, which shocked her mother. Nadene tilted her head all the way around to face that bus driver, directly in his face, & asked sympathetically, "Was your coffee too hot? Did it burn your tongue & make you crabby?" He smiled & patted her hand.

1950

Most children love pretty colors, but Nadene's bright red hair made her more aware of color then the other kids in kindergarten class. She looked best in blues & greens & yellows & browns, but her rosy cheeks made red & purple & bright pink look ugly on her. So, we bought her red boots & purple pajamas — & painted her bedroom pink.

But, her teacher said, "Nadene loves red so much that she caresses the red sweaters & shirts of the other kids.

I had to find fabric that had small red designs, such as tiny apples in a fruit pattern. Then, every day she begged to wear her red tights. I ended up buying her three pairs so she could wear them constantly. Her un-red clothing got pushed to the back of the closet & dresser drawers. Not many people realize what a vital role colors play in children's lives, especially little red heads. P.S. When she was 10, she announced one day, "Red hair is not red – it's partly orange or gold or rust color – why do they call me RED HEAD?" Who knows?

1951

The summer that Ron was one year old & Nadene was five, we made a short trip to visit a small town in mid-Michigan. After only one day, we decided to leave. Even the stop at a gift shop became too hectic. On the trip home, the baby slept, & Nadene sang for about 50 miles. I kept looking back at them...& then became curious. What was keeping her so busy & so happy for so long? She was wrapping & unwrapping something in cleansing tissues, but I couldn't see what it was. Then, I turned & asked, "Nadene, whatcha' got in that little bundle, Honey?"

"Well, Mommy, you've got a baby to wrap up and now I've got a baby I can wrap up!" and she held up a tiny papoose, that she had kidnapped from the six inch Indian momma doll in the gift shop.

Oh! My, it was difficult to explain, that stealing was more important than the tears she shed at losing HER new baby. We finally convinced her that the momma doll would feel sad too, if she were a real momma. Agony at five is real too.

But, it wasn't wise to drive back those 50 miles. So, she hugged her kidnapped baby doll till we got home. Then, we found a small box, wrapped the baby doll lovingly, & mailed it back to the gift shop.

It was a bit more complicated to help a five year old write an apology & a promise to include in the box. NO more stealing, or kidnapping, ever!

1952

People believe that it's common for most baby girls to learn to speak clearly before most baby boys do. Little Nadene spoke in clear sentences the day she was born...(or was it week a later?) - so it seemed.

But, we were not prepared for our smart little Ron. He could put three jigsaw puzzles together at one time, so we did not doubt his intelligence, but, when he kept asking for "Buptee wi ree rees!" & was annoyed, we were bewildered. He was two & a half.

So, a new routine developed in our family. I would ask, "Nadene, what is Ron asking for?" She would very casually say, "He sez cupcake with raisins...he wants a muffin." After she translated, she seemed annoyed at us, too.

Bob & I decided we needed to take more time, & patiently help Ron to learn those bothersome words. So, I said, "Ron, say CUP," he said

"CUP." Then I'd add, "now say CAKE," & he did. "Now, dear say, "CUPCAKE," and he'd say "Bupptee," with a big smile of triumph.

One day Ron tugged on my arm & kept insisting, "Fetter...safe ent!" When Nadene came in the house, I asked her to translate.

"Oh, Mama, he wants his sweater, so he can go down in the basement to play. Why don't you listen to him?" she asked.

So I again tried. "Ron, say BASE." He did. Then I added, "Say MENT." He did. Then I slowly said, "NOW, Honey, say BASE MENT." He grinned & said, "SAFE-ENT."

One morning a few weeks later, Ron was smiling & shaking hands with the man behind our grocery cart, while I placed the items on the checkout counter. The man asked him his name. Ron then stated, "When I was a ootie boy, I called my sister a ootie doyle. Now I'm not ootie, I'm a big boy. Now I call her a lllllllllittle girrrrl." Sincere victory on his face!

Three people behind us clapped. Ron, smiled till bedtime, as he just kept rolling his tongue around the LLLLLLITTLE.

We celebrated when he soon conquered all those hard words & needed no translator.

But, the question Nadene asked stuck in my mind; "Why don't you listen?" I'm sure we need to listen to lotsa' folks lotsa' times, and we need to work on it.

1954

The trolley cars & Chinatown were thrilling, but in San Francisco we had the amazing Pacific Ocean & Fisherman's Wharf still ahead of us. Eight year old Nadene & four year old Ron were silent & wide-eyed as we viewed huge ships & crashing waves.

Daddy asked, "What shall we eat, kids? Want a hamburger?" "Oh no, Daddy, we gotta' have some of those fishes they were ketchin!"

From the menu, Ron was eager to order turtle soup, & Nadene's eyes glowed as she chose Abalone steak. As the waitress set the soup in front of Ron, he stared & then his chin quivered. "What's the matter, dear?" I asked. "There's no turtles in my soup!" How do you repress a smile while explaining that?

A moment later Nadene's fish steak brought a tear to her eyes. She was not prepared for the lovely white piece of fish in front of her. It was not steak. Those Michigan kids just should've been warned, but their parents didn't know what to tell them. What do people from the Great Lakes area know about Pacific sea food? Our shrimp was different than we expected, but we didn't cry.

1955

When Ron was five, he chased his babysitter all over the house with a dead spider on the end of a fly swatter. That was 58 years ago. He recently learned her married name & called her in Michigan from California to apologize for terrorizing her. She was delighted.

1956

When kids are tiny we watch them constantly. By the time they're six you expect to be able to hang clothes on the line while they play nearby. At least I did.

But Ron & his li'l buddy, Mark, slipped in & out of the fenced-in yard so fast, yeah, faster than I could blink.

I put the last clothespin on the sheet & ran to the front yard to find them.

"Ron, Mark, where are you?" I called. No answer. I looked on all sides of the house & yard. Nothing.

"Oh, Ron, what are you doing under the porch? Ron, do I see fire?"

I grabbed the garden hose & turned it full force on the fire & both boys.

They had found matches in a folder, curiosity set in, & they decided to hide under the wooden front porch to experiment. They wondered what leaves would look like if they were on fire. They didn't realize that they couldn't just burn one leaf. OOPS!

By the time I saw the glow of the fire between the slats (or the "skirt" of the porch) the boys had just discovered it was out of their control.

They emerged soaking wet & terrified. I didn't need to say much. When we reached the back yard, both boys had heads down & eyes brimming with tears, I said, "Sit down on the steps while I think."

After all, curiosity isn't a sin, but it can be deadly. We three sat in silence.

Ron asked, "Momma, how can we find out if stones burn?" Good question.

We agreed on a plan.
1. Never again would they light matches without an adult, till they were 27.
2. I found a large size juice-can, & stored it under the sink. On top of it we placed a metal pie plate.

3. Together we would test anything they brought. They brought stones, ice, crayons, mud, wire, & rubber bands, but I refused to burn a lady bug. It lasted for days & days & days & days.

Later, Bob asked Ron to help him burn the trash. About a month later, Bob watched Ron burn the trash. When laws prevented the process of trash burning. Bob remarked, "Perhaps those experiences prevented him from becoming an arsonist, whada'ya think?"

1956

Most parents wonder what their kids are thinking...& I often wonder what our kids think about us. At six, Ron burst in after Sunday school shouting, "Mama, Mama, I know what you are! My teacher sez you're a courager cuz you courage people!" We learned that his teacher had explained & listed the virtues & gifts that God gives people, or helps them to acquire. I felt quite humble & honored by the idea. I asked Ron what he felt his Daddy was. "Oh, he's just the best Daddy & that's all he ever needs to be." We wondered what Ron thought later as he grew up. He now sez "I love you," & that's all we need to know.

1956

In that rented house, no one ever used the front door. It was open to a busy street. When the doorbell rang, I rushed to the front door, knowing it was a stranger. A tall man stood on the porch, holding our six year old son, Ron, by the back of his coat collar. Ron looked terrified, as he somewhat hung from that man's strong grip.

Because the door was used so seldom, it was difficult to get it unlocked & open. "Does this belong to you, Ma'am?" was the man's abrupt & loud question. "Yes sir, what's the problem?" I asked, wondering how to rescue my son.

"Well, he & his buddy threw snowballs at my car, & hit the windshield. That's too dangerous to ignore, so I thought you should know — & keep him out of JAIL!" He frowned at Ron & added, "I'm an off-duty policeman – are you EVER going to do that again, young man?" he asked sternly.

"NO SIR, NO SIR, OH-NO!" was Ron's instant response. We wish there were more men who took the time to train kids, early. I thanked him profusely, as he & I both grinned, & I locked the front door.

1958

Ron was always a climber. At two, he was up & down the steps constantly. We chose not to use a gate. He never fell. He never got into mischief upstairs, and the steps really kept him out of other kinds of trouble. He was fascinated with ladders, but, we did limit him to the smaller one, till he got older & found ways to need the taller one.

"Mom, let me get that platter down for you," became a familiar phrase. He was glad that his Mom was short.

When Ron was eight, we went to visit Yosemite National Park in California, with my sister's family. The men walked ahead of the kids & the women. That worked fine, till Ron burst ahead of everyone, & disappeared over a ledge! Some of those mountains are hundreds of feet above the valley floor − Why are those men just standing there? Where is Ron? PANIC!

The girls & I ran those 20 feet to discover that Ron had jumped down to another ledge, about four feet below the one his Dad & Uncle were standing on. There was no cause for concern − except to those of us who were alarmed at his abrupt jump. I nearly fainted, but we all laughed instead, & decided to sit down & eat lunch to regain our composure. We agreed that, even though eight year old boys can be a pain in the neck sometimes, we don't want them to fall off a cliff.

1960

We've all seen tiny little girls sit on a chair sketching on paper or coloring book with crayons grasped tightly, creating lovely pictures of trees & sunshine. They look so cute. Ours looked especially cute as she wore a pair of adult size plastic eyeglass frames. The glass centers were missing, but the frames set far down on that tiny nose, making every one smile, as we watched her serious expression. The scribbles on the page were typical of a two year old's attempts. Big brother asked, "What does that say, sweetie, I can't read it?"

She whipped off the big frames, handed them to him & announced, "Here, put my glasses on so you can read it."

1960

A fenced-in back yard, & a ten foot square sand box filled with new white sand & oodles of toys, seemed to be enough to keep our two year old happy. Her little play-mates loved it all — but, for some unknown reason, Linda had a desire to sneak out the gate to play in the fine gravel at the end of our driveway. Dangerous.

My kitchen window was only a few feet away, so, each time I would bring her back, scold or explain, or both, & then threaten her with a spanking "next time". Well, finally, the third time, I felt I just had to pop her little butt, to prove I meant it.

The old saying, "This hurts me more than it hurts you," was truly true. She certainly cried, & so did I, but I concealed my tears, & led her back to the lovely sandbox.

Linda sat sullen & silent on the side of her beautiful sandbox, as her friends played & ignored her.

Ron, her ten year old "Big brother," returning from school, picked her up. Hugging & swinging her in a circle, he asked, "Hey, baby doll, why do you look so sad?"

"Momma, hit me on the back of my tummy & it hurt!" then she added, "Honey-Ronny, go get me some spite-amens to take the hurt away, OK?"

Ron confronted me to ask why; quite protective of his sweet li'l dolly. But when he heard the whole sad tale, he also warned her of the danger AGAIN.

We then tried to interpret her request and agreed, the only meds she ever knew about were vitamins, but she must've heard from someone about aspirins as pain killers.

I watched her ever more carefully, and she stopped trying to escape.

NO more need for "SPITE'-AMENS" or spankins' on the back of her tummy.

1961

"Oh! I can't hold the door, Ron!" Three year old Linda screamed to her brother. "It's just the wind, Honey," he answered. "Well, its winding me right off the porch!" – Everyone smiled.

1961

We all enjoyed the ride across the majestic "Big Mac", the bridge that connects Michigan's upper & lower peninsulas.

The kids were glued to the windows in the back seat. Bob & I were far more impressed with the huge structure than they were. Three year old Linda asked big brother, "What are all those funny white lines in the water?"

"Silly, those are waves," he was disgusted at her lack of knowledge, &

at least he wanted her to recognize how smart he was. "Well, anyway...
they're waving at ME, not you!" was her answer with a sarcastic smirk.

1962

Daddy had worked 15 hours the day before, & we all tried to quietly
allow him to "sleep-in". Finally, Linda risked sneaking in to see if he
was ever gonna' wake up. "Daddy, are you in there?" she asked, as she
lifted his eye-lid. "No, this is a big hungry bear!" Her Daddy growled.
Giggles, giggles, hugs & more hugs.

"OK for you," she announced. "I just wanted to know if this was the
day you're going with me to buy my piano?" She hopped over, kissed
him & added, "No, you can't go today, your cheeks are too fuzzy."

1962

When Linda was four, she saw a tree with lovely pink blossoms. It so
thrilled her, she shrieked, "Daddy, when I grow up, I'm gonna buy a
tree like that with a big house next to it. OK? It looks just like pink
popcorn, huh, Daddy?" For her sixth birthday, Bob bought her that
kind of tree, but it took too many months to "turn pink", and she
almost gave up. One morning, about six a.m., she came in, jumped on
her Daddy in bed, & yelled, "You are the most wonderful Daddy in the
world! How did you guess that my very own tree would turn pink?"
That was over 50 years ago, & he often sent her a foto to California of
her tree & said "Hey sweetie, it still turns pink!"

1962

As my friend enjoyed a bite of cake, she asked "Betty, this banana
cake is so fluffy & good. Did it come from a box?" "Oh no, it's my
Mom's old recipe, made from scratch," I answered. Young Linda
pensively asked, "Momma, do you buy scratch in a bag?"

1964

There was never much time to sew "fancy" things for our first two
kids. But, I decided to make our third child a very special dress for her
sixth birthday.

It took hours to choose fabric, trims, buttons & just the right pattern.
None of these in my two drawers full of patterns would do. Even tho'
I'd been sewing for a hundred years, it took extra time & effort – cuz
this li'l dress was gonna' be special.

55

Linda loved it. She said it made her feel like a princess, "Cuz the skirt goes round & round when I dance in circles." The deep aqua trim & buttons matched the lovely print fabric perfectly. Everyone at her birthday party made a big fuss over her, as she floated around in circles.

Actually, she tried to wear that dress every day to school, and wondered why she couldn't, even when it had to be laundered.

Two weeks later, Linda marched in after Sunday school, with a large paper sack, opened it wide, & set it on the floor in her bedroom. She declared, with great determination, "I've got lotsa' nice clothes & those poor kids in Haiti & in Detroit have nothing nice, so I'm sharin' with them."

She nearly emptied her drawers of sox & underwear, saying, "I better save some for me to wear to school...."

Then, she abruptly turned to the closet & pulled down more than half of her dresses, including the new one. I stood in awe & silence wondering how to stop this "runaway train, heading full speed down the track."

No matter how I urged caution, she was still grabbing things. I did convince her she needed extra shoes. At long last she stopped, & I said, "Yes, Honey, I do agree we should share, but must it be your very best, even the new dress I just made?"

"Oh, Mommy, think how happy it will make some little girl. Won't she be happy that you love her too? Just like Jesus does!"

No way to fight that – we bought Linda new sox & pajamas...& hoped that the special dress would fit the special little girl in Haiti or Detroit.

1966

Gram Hazel decided the family should go together to a Walt Disney comedy. It was a challenge to settle on a day & time between Dad's work schedule, the Boy Scout meeting, & Choir practice.

As the six of us settled in one row, the movie started; just in time. For all the coats & hats to be removed, & stashed, we had to steal moments & not miss the film that had already begun. Lotsa' laughter – great fun – but eight year old Linda was crying! Everyone else was laughing.

"Linda, what's wrong? Why are you crying?" Daddy asked. "Oh! Oh! Daddy, I put my hair in my mouth & forgot I was chewing gum. Momma said not to put my hair in my mouth. NOW she'll cut all my hair off cuz it's full of gum!"

She didn't enjoy the film & surely didn't laugh much. -- Big brother teased her, telling her she'd be bald — bad brother! Mom did cut part of the hair off, that was full of gum, but her lovely red curls were all back in a few months. I doubt if she ever put her hair in her mouth again.

1966

That same son never ever fell off ladders or steps (or cliffs) till he turned 16. In our back yard, Ron decided to climb up, to retrieve a little neighbor boy's kite out of a small, but very bushy tree. He reached out toward the end of the branch...couldn't reach that silly kite...reached further...OOPS! The kite, the branch & Ron hit the ground simultaneously. As the doctor wrapped Ron's broken arm, Ron grumbled, "Wouldnja' think I could've done this at six, like normal, kids do?"

22 MOVES TO OUR FIRST HOME

In 1963 we had been married 20 years & had moved 21 times. During WWII the army had moved my 1st Lt. bridegroom & me to 14 different towns & cities all over central Texas. Back in Detroit we lived with my sister & her hubby awhile to help complete their home; then we shared a house with two other couples; then we lived behind a retail store we bought (& soon sold as "honest failures"); then we rented two houses in Detroit; then Bob's job moved him to Saginaw where we rented two more houses...and FINALLY we bought a brand new two-story house. WOW! OUR HOME.

We had three children & my "Mother-in-love" (she never said Mother-in-law) lived with us, so the 4 bedrooms were a blessed necessity. The 2-car attached garage, full basement, full dining room & a "real" fireplace were cause for excitement. But, we were even more excited to pay only $21,900 for all those thrills in a good neighborhood near schools & stores. Double WOW!

We moved in on Maunday Thursday. March winds, rain & sleet blew thru all the open doors. The furnace burned all day but the house never got above 50 degrees.

When our teenager came home from school with a 103 degree fever, we piled lotsa' blankets in the bathtub for her to sleep on to stay warm in the bathroom, till the moving van left. An hour later I was shocked to find that bathroom was frigid! No heat was possible, as the register had never been cut thru the wood behind it. Two heating pads helped till we got to the doctor.

When our treasures were unloaded & the doors were closed none of us could get warm, so we lit a fire in the fireplace. In a few seconds we realized there was no exit for the smoke & the room turned blue. Choking & coughing, open the doors.

On Friday, things began to feel a bit more calm, normal... (whatever that is) as we prepared for three family members scheduled to arrive on Saturday from Detroit, to stay overnite & celebrate Easter with us. Rush, rush, shop, cook, sort, & make up beds for nine people.—PHEW!

We laughingly ignored the light switch for the front porch that turned on the dining room light, & the doorbell that didn't work.

After Sunday breakfast, it was challenging for nine of us to prepare for church in that frigid bathroom, with an electric heater. On Saturday, I had made caramel pudding & salads, so we put the ham & scalloped potatoes & candied yams in the oven to bake while we were at church.

As we re-entered the house there were no familiar aromas from the kitchen. Bob rushed to turn off the gas oven shouting, "Open the doors, air this place out! The gas oven didn't light!" So we cooked our dinner on the top of the stove, on the burners that did light, amid the laughter & groans, "I'm hungry—Let's eat!"

Our rich Auntie loaded the prized dishwasher cuz she knew how & we didn't. The kids squealed & danced at all the noise & steam; a REAL dishwasher. It stopped & Auntie showed us how & why to open the door cautiously. Then, she shrieked, "Man the lifeboats! All that water is still in there!" We all burst out laughing again. Those dishes were very clean & hot & wet.

Four days had been filled with high adventure, so, when our guests left we fell exhausted into our beds. About three hours later a loud noise shook us all bolt-upright out of our beds. All six of us darted into the hall & stood staring at each other in pure shock! Again...it sounded like a gun shot. Over our heads the trap door leading to the attic was lifted & slammed down by those strong March winds. As we all screamed & then laughed, Bob raced to get a ladder & a brick, which he placed on that trap door so we could all go back to sleep, if only the kids would stop giggling.

Monday morning the builder's secretary said they'd come in 10 to 12 days to fix all the problems. I quietly assured her we could tolerate all the others if they'd only fix the heater in the main bathroom &

anchor that noisy trap door. She explained it was impossible. I softly explained I knew the builder's home fone number, & each time it crashes & wakes us all up I'd call him. In a half hour the repair men appeared to solve the two main problems and a week later they fixed all the other "stuff". Our new house became our first home, a truly wonderful home that we've lived in for 51 years. Our great granddaughter said, "Gram, don't ever sell this home, it's truly the nicest home ever!" We agree.

LISTEN...(BY: The Christophers)

In the opera, Pagliacci is a clown whose antics mask a broken heart.

In studying the comic personality, New York psychologist Dr. Samuel Janus says that professional comedians are sometimes basically very sad.

"If one listens to their routines," says Dr. Janus, "many are really crying out loud."

Dr. Abraham Schmitt, author of "Art of Listening With Love," says that such   listening can transform people and relationships.

"This kind of listening," he says, "can free the speaker to search deeper and deeper for a more full understanding and admiration of himself. Listening is then a great act of love at that moment, for it makes the other person more whole."

In North Dakota, a volunteer program, FRIENDS, operates on the theory that no one can understand a personal crisis as well as someone who has had the same experience.

FRIENDS provides a statewide network of nearly 2,000 caring people. The organization has helped in crises related to death, marital troubles, parent-child stress, medical problems and loneliness.

In each case, a "hurting person" is matched with a volunteer who can understand and who will listen.

A Connecticut woman recognized that her talkative mother-in-law was lonely. On a long drive they had to make together, she decided to listen for as long as the older woman needed to talk. The monolog lasted as long as the drive. Exhausted, the daughter-in-law realized she had to be more sensitive to her own needs.

"I knew that after a while I wasn't listening any more," she said. "I wasn't helping her and I was being hard on myself. A martyr doesn't make a good listener."

A gossip was telling a well-known Hollywood actress all about the marital difficulties of a couple who had moved in next door.

"Everyone is talking," said the infomer. "Some are taking her part and some, his."

"And," replied the actress, "I suppose a few eccentric individuals are minding their own business?"

A Hartford, Connecticut, television station turned the tables and listened to its audience.

With a show called, "Nobody Ever Asked Me," WFSB pre-empted its prime time broadcasting for three and a half hours to give its viewers, and live audiences in the three cities, a chance to air their needs and interests.

Topics ranged from concern with unemployment to complaints that the station never covered news of what "good children" in the community were doing.

By listening to their audience, the station reaped ideas for program planning and found that ratings for the three and a half hours topped all other stations in the area.

"Great ideas, it has been said, come into the world as gently as doves. Perhaps, then, if we listen attentively, we shall hear, amid the uproar of empires and nations, a faint flutter of wings, the gentle stirring of life and hope."   **Albert Camus**

ARE YOU A GOOD LISTENER?

- Are you eager to learn about other persons, places and things?
- Can you put yourself in the other person's shoes?
- Do you tune in on the speaker's feelings as well as the words being spoken?
- Do you try to overcome your own emotional attitudes and prejudgments?
- Do you work to identify the main ideas, attitudes and feeling

being communicated?

- Do you avoid interrupting? Especially, do you curb the impulse to complete the other person's sentences?
- Do you ever ask for "feedback" on how people rate you as a listener?
- Do you consciously practice listening skills?
- In short, do you listen to others as you would like to be listened to?

The art of listening is a gift you can give, no matter who you are. And you can give it to anyone.

It doesn't cost a cent. Yet, to a person who needs a listener, it's a gift beyond price. Each of us can start today, wherever we find ourselves, to learn to listen.

> Teach me to listen, Lord,
> To those nearest me,
> My family, my friends, my co-workers.
> Help me to be aware that
> No matter what words I hear,
> The message is,
> "Accept the person I am, Listen to me."
> Teach me to listen, Lord,
> To those far from me –
> The whisper of the hopeless,
> The plea of the forgotten,
> The cry of the anguished.
> Teach me to listen, Lord,
> To myself.
> Help me to be less afraid,
> To trust the voice inside –
> In the deepest part of me.
> Teach me to listen, Lord,
> for Your voice –
> in busyness and in boredom,
> in certainty and in doubt,
> in noise and in silence.
> Teach me, Lord, to listen.
> Amen.

In a Wisconsin hospital, music therapist Deanna Edwards went into the room of an elderly man.

"I went in there to sing a song for him," she said, "and he said, 'Your song was fine but I'd rather talk,' I listened to him, and later I wrote this song:

"It's called, 'Who Will Listen?'

"It's been a long, long time since I've said what's on my mind.
Is there someone who will listen to an old man,
Though they've heard the words a hundred times before?
All the stories I have told, like me, are growing old . . .
Doesn't anybody listen anymore?"

Shortly before his death, writer Louis Cassels outlined
what he called a "ministry of listening."
"When a person confides in you, he usually doesn't want
advice. He wants somebody to understand and care about his
troubles.
"When you can't do anything, as when a person is grieving over
the death of a loved one, listening requires a willingness to
suffer silently with the grieving friend, accepting not only the
reality but also the insolubility of his problem."
It is essential, says Mr. Cassels, "to suppress the urge to
voice moral judgments."

An Illinois woman, convinced that most people at social gatherings
don't listen, decided to test her theory.

Engaging in "small talk" at a party, she said cheerfully to another
person, "By the way, just before leaving my house, I shot my husband."
"Oh really?" came the reply. "How nice for you dear."

"My father and I had words this morning," said a small
child, "but I didn't get to use mine."
Doesn't anybody have the time to spare?
I have memories I wish that I could share.
James D. White, author of "Talking With a Child," says
that many children have little chance for actual
conversation with adults. People talk to them, not with
them.

THE PURPOSE

When a Jewish businessman, a Black Presbyterian educator, a Roman Catholic homemaker, and a Baptist sewing teacher meet with others on a regular basis...there must be a good reason.

During the 1960's there was an increased interest in ugly pornography. Not just the normal interest, in the normal issue, of normal sexuality, but the dirty use of very young children, in what became known as kiddy-porn.

Parents & educators all across the country, were seeking ways to protect children from the sick, sad, life-altering results of that destructive mess; while others were eagerly proclaiming their new exhilaration of freedom...losing the restraints, & leaving behind the old-fashioned morality that they declared harmful.

The speaker from a national group of porn-fighters, came to Saginaw, & alerted local citizens to the problems here.

A small unlikely group met to discuss & inform others, but no real decisions were made & no actions taken.

A week later, as Ethyl & I were stuffing envelopes for a county wide fund-raising project, we sat near a large window in a downtown office building, across the busy street from what was called "The dirty bookstore."

At first, we felt disgusted to see well dressed businessmen, & derelicts, leaving with sacks. But then, we were shocked to see small boys (all younger than ten) carrying paper sacks from that store. If they were buying comic books it seems unlikely that they'd be in paper sacks. As we continued to stuff envelopes, we tried not to look.

We presented our discovery to that small group, at their next meeting. They had chosen "Interfaith Citizens Against Pornography" as their name, at first. But, soon shortened it to "Citizens for Decency." They were concerned, but unsure of what to do about the children in the bookstore.

The next morning, Ethyl & I felt the Lord may be leading us to visit that ugly place. We traded clothes, to avoid being recognized by anyone who might see us there. We prayed, "Father, if this is YOU telling us to do this, then we need You to assure us. So, we will expect a parking spot exactly in front of that busy store. Not next door, in front! If we're imagining it, then please, Lord, give us even one red light, or a flat tire, or a train across the track, and...we'll turn around. Thank You, Jesus. Amen."

Every light was green, all the way, the three miles to downtown, on the main street. (In over 40 years since, it's never ever happened again). As we turned the corner, we both felt relief, as we saw no empty parking spaces... & then a car pulled out, leaving room directly in front of that "dirty bookstore." We groaned. YUK!

We felt the Lord must've wanted the two loving Moms to seek ideas for helping all kids, especially those who had not met HIM yet.

Inside the large building, we saw two distinct areas. The front room was calmly businesslike, but through the doorway, the 18 foot long walls were covered, from floor to ceiling, with racks of paper-back books. It just took a moment to sense the feeling & stench of a carpeted sewer.

Those hundreds of books had ugly titles, (not just suggestive, but ugly) & many with photos of small children in acts of fondling & intercourse with adults. Children too young to even KNOW of such acts, let alone be photographed doing them!

I grabbed a book without even looking at it, & ran to pay the $7.00 (which seemed like $700.00 at the time) & bolted for the exit. Ethyl was directly behind me, having done exactly the same thing.

We burst into the car, drove three blocks, pulled to the curb on the wide busy road, parked, & sat crying. What next?

A mile down the road was the Police Station; surely we'd get answers there. We were told to file a Citizen's Complaint, if we had proof. We handed them the book I had purchased. It had the very same title. Ethyl & I were shocked to learn that, out of the hundreds of tacky ugly books, we had both chosen the same book. Different wall, different shelf, same book. Why?

We told the employees at the Police Department, about the small boys leaving with paper sacks. Adults can make their own choices, but kids need our protection. We signed complaints.

A handsome, well dressed, young man sat nearby as we spoke at the counter. He looked respectable, but turned out to be an accused pornographer, owner of many book stores in several cities. Looks are deceiving. He looked like someone's nice young kid brother.

That evening, as I washed dishes, I watched our kids playing & laughing. I cried a sink full of tears. Those precious little kids in the books are losing their childhood giggles. What can we do? "Help us, Lord!"

It was a shock to awaken early with an urge to call the Chamber of Commerce. Never ever thought of them before...not sure what to say. After I gave a brief idea of what we had done...they offered a list of 17 names of area leaders, who "may want to know what's available to kids here." I picked up that list & rushed it to Ethyl's home.

In anger, Ethyl had just torn up her copy of that ugly book into pieces & thrown them out in the trash. We retrieved them, just as the big trash truck was a block away, seventeen torn up pieces. So what? Why were the 17 pieces & 17 leaders significant?

We prayed again...& then composed a simple note to explain "where,-why,-what, - & when," as briefly as possible. In the envelopes to each of the 17 local leaders, we enclosed a portion of that awful book, as the "WHAT" we had described. We later learned it was important, that it came from the matching book, to the one we had left with our legal complaint.

The note explained, "Now that you see what's available to young kids, you may contact either the Police, The Saginaw News, or us. We're not seeking publicity, but are not ashamed or afraid to include our names." We added all the 'fone numbers & made 19 copies.

It was a challenging task to deliver the 17 copies to the 17 leaders, plus letters to the Police & the newspaper office.

Since porn cannot be mailed, we agreed each envelope must be personally handed to the addressee, no exceptions. One private secretary refused to allow us to talk to her boss, insisting she'd give it to him. We quietly & courteously opened the door to his important meeting room, handed him the letter, & slipped quickly out of the office. Our hearts were pounding, but we both knew we had no options.

During the following week, we received 'fone calls from dozens, who got excited & agreed with us. The Police & newspaper officials called to schedule a meeting with the civic leaders to make plans. They all asked if we were trying to put the bookstore out of business. We both assured them that our purpose was to let the community decide how best to protect our children.

Newspaper headlines told the tale, including our names & the "Citizens for Decency" title. We received several 'fone calls during the night, threatening us, "Mind your own business. I can buy porn if I want to!" Ethyl had a brick thrown through her window.

The bookstore owner sued us for conspiring to destroy his business. Nine other people did what we had done...& the lawsuit was for a million dollars.

A Christian lawyer told the police he would defend us for FREE! Envelopes kept arriving at the newspaper office containing dimes, dollars, & even a large check for $1200. for our defense. What next?

At the weekly meeting of the City Council, many petitions were presented with hundreds of signatures, urging "DO SOMETHING!"

BUT no one knew just what to do. The matter was tabled.

A few days later, a Cub Scout troop was returning from a hike. The two Dads, leading the ten boys, didn't notice that two of them saw a box in a ditch. Natural curiosity...the boys tried to empty the box by stuffing the funny looking little books into their pockets, & jackets & then rejoined the group. At home, food & baths & bedtime kept everyone busy. But two empty beds caused some 'fone calls. In a nearby garage, the two boys were found. They had lit a fire in a big barrel, for warmth & light, so they could examine those books from the ditch. No one could even guess how those books of kiddy-porn got in that ditch; fell off a delivery truck perhaps. The two Dads had a challenge to try to explain porn to their young sons...but then...who CAN explain it?

All of these events were made public of course. Shortly after, some of the ugly books were confiscated by the officials, & we were told of our court date. The nine other folks were to join Ethyl & me. It was a questionable honor to be sued for a million dollars. Contributions still poured in for our defense, some from many miles away.

The day of the trial, we all met the Christian lawyer in the corridor, outside the court room. I asked for his definition of "Conspire," explaining that we eleven had just met for the first time. He spoke quietly, briefly to the judge, who pounded his gavel sternly & announced, "CASE DISMISSED!"

Over $4,000 had been received by the newspaper. Some of it was used by the "Citizens for Decency" for literature & tracts that were helpful to parents, schools & churches.

Some of the money was then divided between three cities that were planning large "Fight for Decency" rallies. That became the realization of our REAL PURPOSE.

A few folks complained that we had not closed the bookstore. We assured all who asked, that God hadn't told us to do that. HE told us (& helped us) to alert & inform our leaders, so that the community could take the appropriate action. We did...& they did, all with God's amazing assistance. When the bookstore finally closed awhile later, none of us were sad.

A COOL HOT MEMORY

Ron was very often naughty & very often nice. Some of those times are more memorable than others.

Eleven year old Nadene wanted to make a special treat while Mom drove the ten minutes to pick up Daddy from work. Ron wanted to help Gramma.

Six year olds have more enthusiasm than skill, so he rushed to fold paper napkins. Mom would be happy to see the table all set. Ron put the silverware in the wrong places. Big sisters are always too bossy, but this time it was OK ... & even exciting. It was fun to put the pickle jar on the table. It was fun to set the cottage cheese carton on the table. It was fun to put the butter dish & the catsup on the table...But, the most fun was to bring the two tall green candles in their big brass candle holders, from the living room, & help big sister light them. Gram Hazel stood watching.

"Hey! Here come Momma & Daddy in the driveway – Let's hide & surprise them," Nadene whispered. They did.

Mom & Dad burst in the back door, eager to get out of the bitter cold. The blast of air from the open door, blew across the room, grabbed a folded paper napkin & thrust it over a candle. It flashed immediately to shouts & screams.

Daddy threw the flaming items into the sink. "Oh no! Oh no! Oh no!" Ron & Nadene blubbered & screamed, tears streaming down their faces.

As they groaned & cried & tried to apologize, Mom & Dad decided that laughs & hugs & kisses, & more laughs & hugs & kisses, were the best fixers for the odd scary supper time surprise. Gram was shocked & speechless.

Fifty seven years later, Ron vividly remembers the panic, the fear, and his yearning to please, which could've ended in tragedy, but instead, ended in the joy of real love. Parents need to learn the kind of loving protection that God tries to teach us.

And...how blessed we are that He protects us from fiery paper napkins.

TIME TO RUN

The phone call from the Billy Graham headquarters was truly a mystery. Someone had told someone that I knew a lot of people, so the lady asked if I would, "Please consider the job of Prayer Chairman of mid-Michigan for the Billy Graham movie Time to Run. It's due to be shown four months from now."

The voice was filled with a combination of authority and hope-filled excitement. My doubt and confusion must have puzzled her. After a few moments, she then asked if I would at best agree to locate a place to hold a meeting and invite at least fifty people to attend. She planned it for twelve days later.

When we hung up, I then realized I knew her name, but had no phone number. She intended to arrive and expected to conduct a meeting. Wow! What had I agreed to do? My head was swimming! Who in the world gave her my number? She said she didn't know. Oh, well, the phrase "That was the least of our worries," took on a new meaning.

The next day I began making the zillion phone calls to locate the place to meet. I never knew that half the town could be away from home and the other half could be using their telephones (there was no Call Waiting back then). It was helpful that I had been involved with Church Women United and a few other groups. But my efforts seemed to be a dismal failure and I dreaded facing that lady when she arrived. I wish I had gotten her phone number, then I could tell her about the sad state of responses. Perhaps that's why she never gave me her number...

There is no way to count those phone calls, nor to guess at all the refusals. All of my helpers were as discouraged as I was, but we just kept calling. More refusals. When that evening finally came, we were all shocked as 64 people showed up! The presentation was interesting and that nice young lady seemed pleased. Then she asked for volunteers.

Some folks had busy schedules, some were planning vacations, or surgeries, etc. After we served coffee, everyone left except three ladies and one man. But, two of them would not be available to help, oh woe! I explained to the lady in charge, named Nicky, that I never learned to type and had no office skills, so I had just about done all that I could do.

One of the ladies agreed to help when she returned from her trip to Europe in a month. That was good, but there had to be things done immediately. That one last lady sat quietly and listened. Then, all of a sudden, she (Marlene) said, "Maybe I can ask for time off from work to help a bit." That was encouraging, but not nearly enough. We learned that she was the Pastor's secretary in a large church and was kept very busy. How could she get time off? Not to worry, we had prayed...no, we bathed the entire project in prayer, and I decided it was really no longer my problem, it was His!

It would take hours to explain all the conversations that took place, but, finally Marlene's boss agreed to her taking time off, and her office skills were vital. Next came the finances and supplies. The budget didn't begin to cover even the basics, so, we prayed again. The next day, a phone call told us to come and pick up as much paper as was needed. Thanks again, Father. We composed the letter, located as many addresses as possible from all over central Michigan. We wondered how many responses could we expect...that led to more prayer.

If we only had enough money, it would be helpful to include a self-addressed, stamped postcard, so that people could tell us their interest and willingness to participate. We hoped they would pray in advance and then take part in the final presentation. We purchased 200 postcards, printed data on each one and enclosed them in the 200 envelopes. Dollars were flying out the window with each step we took. We still needed to buy postage stamps for the 200 envelopes. Free paper, free envelopes, I paid for the postcards, but...well...we had to go to the post office the next day. Marlene considered asking her boss, the pastor.

That day I received a letter in my mailbox with a check in it for an unusual amount. Don't folks usually write a check for 25, 50, or 100 dollars? Well, that check was for the exact amount that was needed at the post office, plus, the exact amount that I had spent for the postcards! I can't remember what the total was, but we all cried and laughed. Even the man at the post office said, "Praise the Lord!", out loud.

There were prayer groups established all over our area of the state. The film was successful and well attended. We were all exhausted when it ended, but never, ever, will we forget that it was the Lord's project! We all felt humbly honored that we had a small part in it. We felt the presence of Jesus over and over again!

TRIALS

A friend confessed that as a very small boy, he tried to help his "mama hen's baby." What he had actually done, was to break open the shell when he saw a crack in the egg.

"Wow! That's a baby chick trying to get out of the tough shell." So he tenderly cracked it further attempting to help, of course.

What he was too young to know, was that the process of coming out of that shell, helped the tiny chick to become stronger. It was a necessary, essential part of life.

When the tiny chick did emerge, as an ugly moist little creature, it didn't even resemble the fluffy, busy, cute chick the boy expected, &

shortly, that precious little thing died. How sad. How upset the small boy was. His wise Daddy helped him learn the lesson, and handle the guilt that we all must learn.

Trials are a vital part of life, to make us grow physically, mentally, emotionally, and spiritually ... and sometimes they're even amusing.

"If it's worth having, it's worth working for," was my Dad's favorite saying. And there's much truth in that attitude. We've been told that "owners take better care of things than renters do." Perhaps we need to have the work effort & trials of ownership, to thrive and prosper.

Learning to drive a "stick-shift car," (are they still called that?) Was a challenge for me, & I truly appreciated the newer model more, when we got one. Trials can produce an element of appreciation.

Families have a variety of trials. Some are financial, or health issues, or relationships. My question is: How many times do we try to fix things ourselves, with our limited knowledge & abilities, when the Lord could, & probably would, do it better, quicker, easier?...The right way! Often as a total surprise! In Isaiah 55:8-9 we're told that God's ways are higher & better than our ways.

When we try to FIX IT, like the small boy did, we don't recognize the true scope & all of the ramifications. We often just get in the way. If only we could learn to trust Him, & get out of the way, so HE can do it...RIGHT!

Hannah Whiteall Smith was a writer from the 1800's. In her book "The Christian Secret of a Happy Life" she wrote, "We trust the cobbler more than we trust God. We leave our shoes to be repaired, trusting that he will know what to do...and...do it right. When we take our problems to the Lord, we watch over His shoulder to see that He does it the way we think is best."

Lord, I want to learn that the trials You allow in my life can best be handled by You; I can't FIX IT. You can! In the strong, wise name of Jesus, I pray. Amen.

That should be the end of the story, shouldn't it?

Well, I was sure of Jesus as my Savior, & had decided I wanted Him to be Lord of my life, BUT, I was still walking on egg shells. I was too new in my Christian walk to be strong or stable...I was just learning – lots!

At a Women's Aglow Fellowship meeting in a large auditorium, hundreds of people attended. Dozens responded to an invitation to come forward for prayer. One of the leaders told me they needed me to help!

"I'm not a trained counselor, but I can go with folks in prayer to the

Great Counselor," I said, as we entered the crowded back room. Not nearly enough chairs. People crying, praying, or just watching & waiting their turn for someone to help them.

It took me awhile to gather the courage to approach a young lady who was crying quietly. She & her two sisters were standing next to their father, who was seated.

For two years that dear man had not been able to work at his job, or eat, or sleep properly, because of constant hiccups! He had lost over 60 pounds & looked sick ... pitiful.

I was stunned. How in the world do I pray for that? I first suggested we anoint him with oil (from the large bottle of oil on a central table), and then hold hands. That was simple. What next?

As we four circled that sweet, sad, discouraged man, he continued to hiccup at regular intervals. The first lady briefly told of the many doctors, specialists & the Mayo Clinic where they sought help. We prayed silently, & then began to praise God & ask forgiveness. We confessed bitterness, doubt & unforgiveness in our hearts. We took turns adding to the prayer. All of a sudden, one lady shrieked, "Listen! HE STOPPED!" Sure enough, those dreadful hiccups stopped. We didn't even ask God for healing or deliverance. We praised Him, thanked & confessed. Then, HE DID IT!

Some trials are unexpected & can even be funny...sort of ...

Everyone who owns a home knows that leaves collect in the gutters & need to be removed. Even after Bob turned 75, he still climbed to the roof on a tall ladder, dragging up the garden hose to do that, every year.

He was mowing the grass as I left to do three errands. I assured him I'd be back to fix his lunch. His days off were few & I tried to make them pleasant, so I would hurry back.

My first two errands took so long, I decided to call & tell Bob I'd be delayed. The 'fone didn't answer. He must still be outside. I called the next door neighbor, Don & asked him to give Bob the message, & he, of course, agreed.

When I arrived an hour later both men were sitting on the steps with bottles of pop in their hands, laughing...out loud!

"What's so funny?" I asked.

"It's a good thing you called," Bob answered. "While I was up on that ole' roof, I yanked on the hose, it knocked over the ladder, & I was stranded. Could've been up there all day if Don hadn't come to tell me you called! An hour up there was long enough...sure glad you called Don." They agreed to only climb up on the roof when someone knew it, next time.

That should be the end of the story, but the really truly end (as the kids call it), came when Don did the very same thing a month later. It's good we were home to rescue him.

Our decisions, good or bad, influence our lives. God must grin & say, "They need to think first & act second. When will they learn?"

TRIALS OF MANY KINDS

When Bob & I learned that our state taxes were given to certain private schools, we signed a petition, with hundreds of other folks, who disapproved. If we give to some private schools, we must give to all, & that wasn't a wise use of taxes, needed for public schools. Years passed, & we heard that the system changed.

Several years later, I joined a group, who objected to children being exposed to ugly child-pornography. The "dirty book store" sued us, but the case was dropped, & the problem solved quickly.

Bob managed a large retail store in a chain of upscale stores with headquarters in Detroit. After our three children were in school, I began to teach sewing, tailoring & crafts in stores, schools, & Delta College. So, we stayed busy.

But, our whole family was totally uninformed about legal matters. The world of lawyers & lawsuits was foreign to us.

One day, I was called to jury duty. A whole new world came into focus. Even tho' I was born in Detroit, & spent four years following the Army while Bob served in WWII, I was still basically ignorant about folks who kill & steal. And...I did not want to learn.

There was much to learn about the judicial system. We sat in a large room waiting to be called; just a few were called each day, as the rest waited. It was with mixed emotions, that we waited; we hated to wait, but dreaded the reality of being called to serve on a difficult trial.

At last it was my turn. In the court room, they ask questions of each potential juror. The first question was, "Have you ever been sued?" When I answered, "No," I was abruptly asked, "What about the time you were sued for a million dollars by the book store owner?"

"Oh, I forgot about that, I'm sorry!" I quickly left the room.

The next day the question was "Have you ever sued anyone?" When I said "No," I was again abruptly asked, "What about the time you & your husband sued the State of Michigan?"

"Oh my, I forgot about that too, I'm so sorry!" I rushed back to the waiting room.

OOPS! Do they think I am lying, or stupid...or what?

The next day I was called & the question was, "Do you know any of the people involved in this legal action?" I carefully examined the names, all of them, & honestly said, "No, I do not know any of the people involved!"

It was great to say that with a clear conscience, & be totally innocent this time, after the previous major goofs.

When all the people entered the court room & took their seats, I was shocked. One of them had been in my tenth grade Sunday school class for a full year. But, as I gasped, I realized I did not know her married name...in fact, I did not know her as an adult, so, I never uttered a word. That is, no words aloud, only to the Lord, again. Please, Father, give us all wisdom & understanding.

It came as extreme relief when the case was dropped...& my time on jury duty expired.

Phew! Thank you, Lord!

Recently, my granddaughter took a copy of my first book titled "He Did It" to read while she waited to be called to serve on a jury. A person seated nearby commented on the title...in that setting.

THE MASTER'S VESSEL

The master was searching for a vessel to use
On the shelf there were many. Which one would He choose?
"Take me," said the gold one, "I'm shiney and bright. I am of great value and I do things just right. My beauty and luster will outshine the rest
And for someone like You, Master, I would be best."

The Master passed on with no word at all
He looked at the silver urn, narrow and tall.
"I'll serve You dear Master, I'll pour out Your wine and be at Your table whenever You dine. My lines are so graceful and my carvings so true,
And silver will always compliment You."

Unheeding, the master passed on to the brass, it was wide-mouthed and shallow and polished like glass.
"Here, here," cried the vessel, "I know I will do. Place me on Your

73

table for all men to view."

"Look at me," cried the goblet of crystal so clear. "My transparency shows my contents so dear. Though fragile am I, DON'T CROSS ME.
I will serve You with pride and I'm sure I'll be happy in Your house to abide."

The Master came next to a vessel of wood, polished and carved and it solidly stood. "You may use me dear Master," the wooden bowl said.
"But I'd rather You'd use me for FRUIT, please.. NO BREAD!"
Then the Master looked down and saw a vessel of clay
Empty and broken it helplessly lay. No hope had that vessel that the Master might choose to cleanse and make whole, to fill and to use.
"Ah, THIS is the vessel I've been hoping to find. I will mend it and use it and make it all Mine."
I need not the vessel with pride in itself, not the one so narrow
To sit on the shelf. Not the one that is big-mouthed and shallow and loud; not the one that displays its contents so proud. Not the one who thinks he can do things "just right", but THIS plain, earthen vessel filled with My power and might. Then gently, He lifted the vessel of clay mended it, and cleansed it and filled it that day. He spoke to it kindly, "There's work you must do. You just pour out to others and I'll pour in to you!" – **Author unknown**

SOME TEENS ARE AMAZING

Because I can't even sing Happy Birthday on key...I was thrilled when our little Nadene sang a solo in church when she was six.
Bob's whole family had musical talents. His Mom, our Gram Hazel, who lived with us for twenty years, played the piano so beautifully that the Masonic Temple in Detroit called her to substitute, at times.
Bob's younger brother, Ross was a tenor & sang at the Chicago Civic Light Opera once. His young sister Jeanie sang like an angel. Bob had a beautiful, deep baritone voice.
Nadene sang in choirs & music groups in church, & all thru school. In the 10th grade she won a contest, & was awarded a week at Interlochen Music Camp in northern Michigan. Her pals at school, & all of us, were thrilled with her success.
Two weeks before she was to leave for camp, my sister's husband Carl, was nearly killed in an accident in California. His doctor warned

that he mustn't get discouraged or even bored. He must be kept gently busy...perhaps children could keep him occupied, but not strenuously. My sister called to ask if I'd bring the kids & stay three weeks before Bob's already scheduled vacation, so we'd all return home together.

We suggested Nadene could stay with Gramma, & then after the week at music camp, she could come to CA with her Daddy. She only considered it a few seconds till deciding she just HAD to come & help care for her beloved Uncle Carl. The music camp trip was cancelled.

When the three kids & I reached California, Carl was so weak he couldn't open a pill bottle & needed help to stand up.

Carl loved watching two year old Linda play with the kitty. Ron was ten. He pounded nails to bang a board on a tree trunk so he could chin himself...Carl enjoyed watching him grow stronger each day. Nadene, 15 sang for Carl, made lemonade & waited on him endlessly. After three weeks, Carl had improved so much he could chin himself on Ron's board, & he took walks with the girls.

Bob arrived to spend his ten day vacation, & Carl even joined us on short trips. Nadene felt she'd been a help to Carl, so it was worthwhile to sacrifice her precious week at music camp. The music teacher said, "There's always next year, dear."

Sure 'nuff, Nadene was awarded that wonderful week at Interlochen Music Camp again the following year. In eleventh grade she still qualified. As we sewed name tags in all her required blue shirts, excitement ran high. The suitcase was cleaned out. Her shoes were cleaned & placed in plastic bags. Two more days.

And then, the mail came. One very formal letter came from Interlochen Music Camp. "We're sorry to inform you, there was an error, the camp is full, & there will not be room for you. We are over-booked. Perhaps you will arrange to come next year. If so, please make your reservation in advance." Shock!

Nadene cried, but said nothing. Her young brother Ron, banged his fist on the table & growled, "Aw, that's rotten!" as he burst out the door. We all tried to find the right words...but there just weren't any.

The first week of her senior year at school, the music teacher hugged her & apologized, as though it were her fault. Seniors do not qualify for Interlochen scholarships. They can't bring back to school what they learn at camp. Too bad.

Two weeks later, Nadene was amazed to learn that the entire senior class, & even a few juniors, were organizing a bake sale as part of a fund raiser. Those kids earned enough to send Nadene to Interlochen. WOW! How thrilling, & what a surprise!

The blue shirts (required by the camp) already had name tags. But we were all more excited than ever. The weather was perfect all week & she really liked her roommate. The high-light of her reports to us at home, were that Van Cliburne was there & practiced every day in the area next to their laundry room. The girls dampened the clothes with tears, as they ironed everything twice, for an excuse to stay & listen. He was charming & friendly to them.

Van Cliburne spoke often to the girls & reminded them, "If I skip one hour of my needed practice time, I later know it. If I skip two hours, my teacher knows it. If I skip two hours & ten minutes, everyone knows it!" He praised Nadene's lovely voice, & they were delighted that he took time to listen & talk to them.

Interlochen gives annual prizes & amazing awards to worthy young artists in all areas of music. Nadene won a four year, full-paid scholarship to University of Michigan...& then gave it up to get married.

We're happy to have our precious grandchildren. Nadene's daughter Christine & her son Daniel are married & now live nearby. They bless me constantly.

But there's more to the story. In my first book, "HE DID IT," I told in much detail, the sad, but lovingly sweet, tale of Nadene's life, her music, & her too early death.

During her severe illness, she needed 80 pints of blood. We were surprised & grateful that 17 of the San Diego Chargers ball team donated blood for her. Even tho' she died, we appreciated the good care she had received.

That prompted me to REPAY (if that's even remotely possible to consider) all of that blood. Some folks said it was a quirky, silly idea, so I didn't talk about it; I just donated blood as often as I could, till I reached the ten gallon mark. The folks at the blood center asked, "Why stop now?" So I didn't. They say they'll take blood as long as it runs, & mine still does.

A few years ago I learned of a genuine need for blood donors. Some schools have had successful blood drives, but it does take someone to start the ball rolling. I went to Nadene's high school & challenged them by telling them the story of those kids & their amazing fund-raising efforts. Some of the kids "GOT IT," & the blood drive was a success!

Nadene would've been delighted, & spent the next day singing praises to those teenagers! I would too, if I could sing.

ALL TEENS NEED TO BE:

Our sixteen year old grandson Dan & I sat one day discussing what teens need. Together we made a list. Years later I shared it with his sixteen year old daughter, Danielle. Yes, all teens need to be: Loved, trustworthy, truthful, needed, praised (if earned), respected, aware of other's needs, wanted & included, encouraged, improving, challenged, guided, active, appreciated, heard, creative, involved, disciplined, firmly but lovingly, taught skills & courtesy, grateful, helping others, in healthy friendships, busy at worthwhile things, made aware of Jesus' love!

After reading it again recently, I began to wonder if that list would be different for adults. I am 91 & I still need the same things.

COLLECTABLES – COLLECTIBLES

A few fads? A new interest? An old hobby? A part of your history? Yes, all of that and more. I remember my Gram's box of old thimbles. In our childhood memories, don't we often relive the gentle excitement that came at someone's house when they showed us a teapot collection or some old Indian relics? Old photos certainly become a wonderful collection, as do post cards and baseball cards, ad infinitum.

The age of collector means nothing, but the age of the collected is sometimes crucial. What do you collect?

A few years ago I had the great fun of visiting the army nurse who had delivered our first baby in an Army Camp in Texas in 1945. She and her retired airline pilot husband, now live near Bellingham, Washington. As we all walked along the sandy beaches we were delighted to pick up many agates. But it became even more thrilling to watch my host put those rough, dirty, ugly stones into his revolving machine that changed them into smooth, lovely shaped, gorgeous colored pieces, fit for the finest jewelry. His collection of agates is fascinating and growing constantly.

Now, when I wear a necklace and earrings that our friend made for me of those beautiful stones, it brings back vivid memories of their origin. How can tiny stones of pink, green, or grey, some with streaks of sunlight throughout, be so strong and so important in our world? We're told that only diamonds are harder and stronger than agates, which have seemingly endless uses in industry and personal products.

God's creativity is endless. Seems I take these things for granted. I often remember agates as the marbles we played with, "a hundred years ago." Didn't you draw huge circles in the dirt with a stick, as the kids gathered around for the big game? Then came the trading and the boasting, of course. And such collections we started!

In a National Park near the Washington, Canadian border, a breathtaking display of agates in all colors, forms, and sizes gave me more information than can usually be acquired in a lifetime. The person, who later became famous and wealthy enough to sponsor that exhibit, probably never knew at the start of his great growing collection, how far-reaching the results would be. He couldn't have known that children, teens, and adults from all over the world, and this housewife from Michigan, would experience chills and thrills of wonder and delight while admiring all those agates.

On each of our 8,000 mile Amtrak trips (about 16 of them) we had such limited space in our luggage that we chose not to buy things to bring home. After about six or seven trips we learned that our daughter Nadene, had slipped a small shell in her pocket & then into her suitcase. Each shell was different. We wondered how she remembered how to choose such a variety. When her little brother, Ron snitched on her & told us, it was extremely difficult to explain to her that we break the law when we remove anything from national and state parks & lakesides, without hurting her fragile feelings. So, from then on, we purchased shells for her lovely growing collection. Such variety of size, color & shape. God truly gives us beauty beyond our comprehension. Webster sez we can spell it both ways – maybe he thought that collecting had no limits, as I do.

Sometimes we hear collecting called an art; often it's a hobby or a fad; it could be called contagious, but always, I call it fun.

And now...more of my "collection" of WIT & WISDOM can be shared. YAY!

MORE WIT AND WISDOM

Each night let's turn our tangled lives over to God...He's gonna' be up anyway.

If we love only those who are lovable; If we forgive only those who deserve it; If we hope only for things that are available...where is the virtue in that?

As we celebrate the years behind us, they become stepping stones of strength & joy, & loving, eager, inspiration for the years ahead.

True gratitude comes when we can say "Thanx" for the way things ARE.

Someone blessed me once when she said, "I pray you'll become as beautiful as God meant you to be when He first thought of you."

God has a plan for each of us. We will have hope & exciting encouragement when we learn that hope with no limit is wearing everyday WORK clothes.

When the people complained, it displeased the Lord. Numbers 11:1

"I get tired of hearing people complain about the weather," I commented recently to my brother-in-law.
"So, you are complaining about those who complain about the weather!" he said.
Surprised and trying to defend myself, I replied somewhat arrogantly, "You are complaining about me complaining about those who complain about the weather!" Then we both burst out laughing.
Complaining is contagious and comes in many forms: criticizing, grumbling, finding fault, nagging, whining. The children of Israel complained about God, about Moses, and about their circumstances. When they complained about the manna and asked for meat, God sent quail. God was always trying to please them, but they were never satisfied.

During the memorial service for an eighty-three year old woman, known as Miss Ruby, one of the Ministers described her as one who "knew how to be a blessing." He was right. Whether at home, at church, on the golf course, on a mission trip, in the hospital...even on her deathbed...Miss Ruby knew how to be a blessing. She knew how to encourage. She knew how to make people feel special. She knew how to make them laugh. She knew how to lend a helping hand. She knew how to mentor younger women. She knew how to love people because she knew God loved her. That confidence enabled her to bless the lives of those around her. May that be true of each one of us. Lord teach us how to be a blessing to others, in Jesus' name. Amen.

"These are the ancestors of Jesus Christ," Matthew 1:1

As I've explored my family tree for the last fifteen years, I've discovered some beautiful flowers that have blossomed there. I've also found some real fruits and nuts hanging from the limbs!

When I read the lineage of Jesus, I see what a strange collection of ancestors He had as well. His genealogy line contains liars, betrayer, and thieves, as well as the righteous and godly. Some may find that hard to comprehend, but for me this lineage establishes the frame of reference by which to understand God's love and mercy. Jesus came "to call not the righteous but sinners to repentance" (Luke 5:32). In His genealogy, we see that Jesus came not only for, but also through sinners.

God's grace still reaches people of every kind...rich and poor, beggars and kings, saints and sinners, losers and winners. People like you. People like me.

Abraham begat Isaac: and Isaac begat Jacob, etc...

Whenever I read this genealogy, I think of Ezra Kimball. A Boston shoe clerk, Kimball was also a Sunday school teacher. In 1858 he introduced a young man to Jesus Christ. That fellow, Dwight L. Moody, became an evangelist of international fame. Speaking in London, Moody awakened an evangelistic zeal in the heart of a small church pastor, Frederick Meyer. Meyer, upon visiting an American college campus, introduced Christ to a senior named Wilbur Chapman. Years later, Chapman worked with the YMCA, where he employed a former baseball player to do some preaching. His name was Billy Sunday. Sunday held a revival in Charlotte, North Carolina. The locals were so enthusiastic they planned a second campaign with evangelist Mordecai Hamm. In that revival a young man gave his life to Christ. His name was Billy Graham.

Doesn't that sound familiar? Kimball begat Moody; Moody begat Meyer; Meyer begat Chapman: Chapman begat Sunday; Sunday begat Hamm; Hamm begat Graham; Graham begat ... Who can count the lives touched by that shoe clerk? Some estimate two billion or more!

Prayer: Redeemer God, thank You for those people who have nurtured my faith. Thank You for parents, teachers, pastors, and friends who proclaimed to me the living Word. Use me to "begat" others; in the name of Jesus, Amen.

––––––––––

Preachers are fond of asking the question: "If you were arrested for being a Christian, would there be enough evidence to convict you?" I might ask myself today: Would there be enough evidence to convict me of being an Easter Christian?

If we truly believe in Easter, there must be some evidence of our Easter faith. If we believe that Jesus is risen...and we with Him, then we will somehow stand out from the crowd. People will see the "evidence."

What kind of evidence? For starters, a spirit of joy, the radiance of hope, an attitude of confidence. We all know "doom and gloom" people.

Easter people brim with hope. They see the possibility of new life around every corner. They believe that the crosses of daily life are not dead-ends, but doors to new life. Their values are not those of the culture of death, but come from the gospel of life!

BORROWED

They borrowed a bed to lay His head
When Christ the Lord was born;
     They borrowed the ass in the mountain pass
And He rode despite their scorn.
     But the crown that He wore and the cross that He bore
Were His own –
The cross was His own.
They borrowed the bread when the crowd He fed
     On the grassy mountainside;
He borrowed the dish of broken fish
     With which He satisfied;
But the crown that He wore and the cross that He bore
     Were His own –
The cross was His own.
     He borrowed the ship in which to sit
To teach the multitude;

He borrowed the nest in which to rest,
He never had a home so crude;
But the crown that He wore and the cross that He bore
Were His own –
The cross was His own.
He borrowed a room on His way to the tomb
The Passover Lamb to eat;
They borrowed a cave for Him a grave,
They borrowed a winding sheet;
But the crown that He wore and the cross that He bore
Were His own –
The cross was His own, and
He only needed the tomb for the weekend!

CHRISTIAN BUMPER STICKERS

- Be fishers of Men ...You catch 'em, He'll clean 'em.
- A clean conscience makes a soft pillow.
- A family altar can alter a family.
- Are you wrinkled with burden? Come on into Church for a faith lift!
- Coincidence is when God chooses to remain anonymous.
- Do your best and then sleep in peace. God is Awake.
- Fear knocked. Faith answered. No one was there.
- Forbidden fruits create many jams.
- God doesn't want shares of your life; He wants controlling interest!
- God promises a safe landing, not a calm passage.
- Having truth decay? Brush up on your Bible!
- He who is good at making excuses is seldom good for anything else.
- If God is your Co-pilot –Swap seats!
- We set the sail; God makes the wind.
- We're too blessed to be depressed.
- Wisdom has two parts: 1) having a lot to say. 2) Not saying it.
- You can tell how big a person is by what it takes to discourage him.

TO ELIMINATE BITTERNESS:

1. Make a list of ways you've been offended.
2. List your own faults & offenses.
3. List things God has forgiven you for.
4. Ask God to help you see that person thru God's eyes... as a tool in God's hand...to see that hurt as HE sees it.
5. Ask for true forgiveness in your heart, toward the offender, even if it is all his/her fault.
6. Then ask God to help you remember the way Jesus forgave those who offended Him...& give you that same gracious gift.
7. Write a brief note, or call the person and ask for forgiveness for the bitterness (even if it is All their fault) & do not get bogged down in explanations nor excuses. Very briefly express your love & hang up, or sign your name to the note.
8. Thank God for working thru you to end the bitterness & replace it with HIS love & joy & peace.
9. Then say, "By an act of my WILL, I choose to forgive him/her, in the name of Jesus. Amen."

To live without faith is like driving in a fog.

––––––––

The dilapidated old car wheezed up to the toll gate. "Seventy cents," said the attendant. "Sold," answered the driver wearily.

––––––––

"And now, children," said the harassed woman to a wild group at her small son's Christmas party, "there will be a special prize for the one who goes Home first."

––––––––

The light that shines farthest shines brightest at home.

––––––––

I read somewhere that Winston Churchill said something like, "We make a living by what we get, but we make a life by what we give."

—————————

We hear about Paul's 'thorn in the flesh.' When we have a thorn we rush to remove it. Jesus had many thorns—in HIS crown.

—————————

The only people you should try to get even with are those who have helped you.

—————————

Why is it that when we speak to people it's for their own good, but when people speak to us, they're interfering?

—————————

Happy people rarely think of happiness. They're too busy making others happy, by service or sacrifice.

—————————

The famed Bolshoi Ballet began 200 years ago in a Moscow orphan asylum, and its first performing ballet company consisted of 62 orphans.

—————————

When we float around in the sea of life & fear, we will drown in our problems; the best life preservers are God's promises.

—————————

As we read & talk about those who ran after Jesus, I wonder how many did it for miracles & how many did it for the loaves.

—————————

Two things are hard on the heart: Running up stairs and running down people.

———————

He who watches the clock will always be one of the hands.

——————————

I read "The meek will inherit the earth. But—they prob'ly won't find a parking space."

——————————

The more you know & the more you need, the more you'll kneel.

——————————

The pursuit of excellence is gratifying & healthy.
The pursuit of perfection is frustrating & neurotic,...As well as a terrible waste of time & energy—and even treasured friendships.

———————

A careless word may kindle strife.
A cruel word may wreck a life.
A bitter word may hate instill.
A brutal word may smite & kill.
A gracious word may smooth the way.
A joyous word may light the day.
A timely word may lessen stress.
A loving word may heal & bless.

———————

A little flattery isn't too bad if you don't inhale it, or even believe it.

———————

NUGGETS FOR THOUGHT

Live so that when you tell someone you are a Christian, it confirms their suspicions instead of surprising them.

—————

DAILY EXERCISES
1. I will secretly do a good deed & not get found out.
2. I will do two things I don't want to do.
3. I will not show anyone when my feelings are hurt.

—————

They say good judgment comes from experience, but experience comes from poor judgment.

—————

The difference between education and experience is really quite simple: Education is what you get from reading the fine print. Experience is what you get from not reading it.

—————

There is very little difference in people, says Clement Stone, but that little difference makes a big difference. The little difference is attitude. The big difference is whether it is positive or negative.

—————

The shortest distance between two points has a DETOUR sign on it.

—————

Dirt comes in two colors: dark dirt shows up best on light objects; & light dirt is attracted to dark objects.

—————

If you're looking for a good way to manage your day—Take a free moment in the morning & bury your telephone.

—————

Remember when the only tanning parlor in town was the woodshed?

IMPORTANT RECALL NOTICE

The maker of all human beings is recalling all units manufactured, regardless of make or year, due to the serious defect in the primary and central component of the heart. This is due to a malfunction in the original prototype units code named Adam and Eve, resulting in the reproduction of the same defect in all subsequent units. This defect has been technically termed, "Sub-sequential Internal Non-morality," or more commonly known as SIN as it is primarily expressed.

Some other symptoms:
a. Loss of direction
b. Lack of peace and joy
c. Depression or confusion in the mental component
d. Foul vocal emissions
e. Selfish, violent behavior
f. Amnesia of origin
g. Fearfulness
h. Rebellion

The Manufacturer, Who is neither liable nor at fault for this defect, is providing factory authorized repair and service free of charge to correct this SIN defect. The Repair Technician, Jesus, has most generously offered to bear the entire burden of the staggering cost of these repairs.

There is no additional fee required. The number to call for repair in all areas is P-R-A-Y-E-R. Once connected, please upload your burden of SIN through the REPENTANCE procedure. Next, download ATONEMENT from the Repair Technician, Jesus, into the heart component.

No matter how big or small the SIN defect is, Jesus will replace it with:
1. Love
2. Joy
3. Peace
4. Kindness
5. Goodness
6. Faithfulness

7. Gentleness
8. Patience
9. Self-control

Please see the operating manual, HOLY BIBLE, for further details on the use of these fixes. As an added upgrade, the manufacturer has made it available to all repaired units a facility enabling direct monitoring and assistance from the resident Maintenance Technician, the Holy Ghost. Repaired units need only make Him welcome and He will take up residence on the premises.

WARNING: Continuing to operate the human being unit without corrections voids the Manufacturer's warranty, exposing the unit to dangers and problems too numerous to list and will result in the human unit being permanently impounded.

For free emergency service call on JESUS!

DANGER: The human being units not responding to this recall action will have to be scrapped in the furnace. The SIN defect will not be permitted to enter Heaven so as to prevent contamination of that facility.

Thank you for your attention.

Please assist where possible by notifying others of this important RECALL NOTICE.

Author unknown

IF JESUS PROMISED

If Jesus promised to provide
Just like the Bible said,
Why do we still worry
About our daily bread?

If our steps are ordered
And directed by God's hand,
Why do we continue to
Put our trust in man?

If we believe that Jesus
Deserves our time each day,
Why is time an issue
When we worship and pray?

If He said He'd never fail
Or leave us all alone,
When will we stop struggling
To make it on our own?

If He cares for sparrows
And knows if one should fall,
When will we remember that
He loves us most of all!?

_____

The truth often costs a lot. But, it still costs less than hiding or altering it.

_____

The knowledge that someone, anyone—whether it be Paul or the Host of Heaven or my best friend—is praying for me, makes the air around me shimmer with possibility. I am blessed, I am awed, and I am strengthened. One who intercedes is most like Christ; one who intercedes for me reminds me that Christ has commissioned others to Pray for me.

We thank you, God, for those who have prayed for us from the day of our birth until now.

_____

"Lord, help me to live from day to day
In such a self-forgetful way
That even when I kneel to pray
My prayer shall be for others."
Billy Graham

OPTIMISTS TEND TO ENJOY HEALTHIER, LONGER LIVES

Hey, look on the bright side. If you do, you might just live longer. And, chin up, pal: you could become an optimist.
Researchers at the Mayo Clinic in Rochester, Minn., have confirmed

what many people already believe: Optimists tend to live longer, healthier lives. Researchers looked at a group of 839 patients who had taken a personality test.

The study found that expected survival rate and the pessimists had a 19 percent increase in the risk of death.

Researchers could not explain how pessimism is associated with a risk of early death, but suggested a mind-body link or an attitude toward medical care, with optimists more positive in seeking and receiving medical help.

Robert Thayer, a professor of psychology at California State University, Long Beach, is the author of a book. "The Origin of Everyday Moods." Thayer said most people think of optimism and pessimism as fixed traits. But he and his colleagues find that feelings of optimism and pessimism tend to come and go – like moods.

"When we're feeling energetic and calm, we feel optimistic," he said. Feeling tense and tired turns us into pessimists.

Thayer said so-called born pessimists may be genetically predisposed to a bleaker outlook, but that even these people can buck up by becoming aware of their energy state and managing it. Exercise can help tremendously, he has found, and it doesn't have to be a full-tilt workout. A brisk, 10 minute walk, he said, can boost optimism.

Optimism is a habit that can be acquired.

Concentrate on what they want in life, not what they don't want. Optimists, he said, focus on solutions. Rather than problems. In other words, switch from "I hate my boss" to "What can I do to build my career?" Once people decide what they want, they should spend more than half their time pursuing their goals.

It's best, he said, to avoid "emotional vampires." These are people who "suck the good feelings right out of your skull" by complaining, moaning and blaming. Adopt the straight posture and brisk stride of the optimist, use upbeat language (don't say you're "tired," say you're "recharging") and let others see you acting optimistically.

Helping others can help build optimism. Pessimists are often those who believe they must be self-reliant and aggressive toward others. Optimists, he said "Discover that cooperation is better than competition." 12-step recovery programs are built on the idea of healing by helping others heal. He suggested getting a new attitude by performing some community service.

"Here's something you can do" Give away your time," he said. "Do something that's helpful."

Garret Condon

90

Resilient people are like trees bending in the wind. They bounce back.

Pessimism & Optimism are the terms given by the world. Victims & victors are terms given by the WORD of God. In John 10:10—Jesus said, "I am come that they might have life, and that they might have it more abundantly."

In Philippians 4: 4-8 we're told some ways to help us achieve that life style! "Rejoice in the Lord always: and again I say, Rejoice. Let your moderation be known unto all men. The Lord is at hand. Be careful for nothing; but in every thing by prayer and supplication with thanksgiving let your requests be made known unto God. And the peace of God, which passeth all understanding, shall keep your hearts and minds through Christ Jesus. Finally, brethren, whatsoever things are true, whatsoever things are honest, whatsoever things are just, whatsoever things are pure, whatsoever things are lovely, whatsoever things are of good report; if there be any virtue, and if there be any praise, think on these things." And verses 12 & 13 say "I know both how to be abased, and I know how to abound: every where and in all things I am instructed both to be full and to be hungry, both to abound and to suffer need. I can do all things through Christ which strengtheneth me."

And then I Corinthians 15:57 & 58 says "But thanks be to God, which giveth us the victory through our Lord Jesus Christ. Therefore, my beloved brethren, be ye stedfast, unmoveable, always abounding in the work of the Lord, forasmuch as ye know that your labour is not in vain in the Lord.

"WHY BE AFRAID OF AGING?

Why are we so afraid of age, and why do we lie about it? Whenever I am asked my age, I always flat out tell the truth. It's beautiful to reach the age where you can quit pressing to prove yourself, where you can be your own self, the person God created, with no apologies.

If I only looked at the women's magazines and fashion pages, I suppose I would become despondent about this relentless march of the years; however, I look to the Scriptures and find that aging has very high priority. That's good news.

We cannot demand respect, but we should command respect

because of our love and fear of Almighty God and our example of godly living.

In Leviticus 19, the Bible talks about showing fear of God by standing up in the presence of elderly people and showing respect for the aged.

How far we have strayed from Biblical principles! In the patriarchal times, the older people were the center of family life. They were the ones who gave the advice and led Israel in times of trouble. Look at the priests, the judges, and the warrior; they were admired and revered.

In Proverbs 16, the Bible says that old age is not a curse, it's a prize. It states that gray hair is a crown of glory, gain by living a godly life.

Old age is not a burden, it's a reward.

————————

"A DAY OFF"

So you want the day off. Let's take a look at what you are asking for.

There are 365 days per year available for work. There are 52 weeks per year in which you already have two days off per week, leaving 261 days available for work. Since you spend 16 hours each day away from work, you have used up 170 days, leaving only 91 days available. You spend 30 minutes each day on coffee break that accounts for 23 days each year, leaving only 68 days available. With a one hour lunch period each day, you have used up another 46 days, leaving only 22 days available for work. You normally spend 2 days per year on sick leave. This leaves you only 20 days available for work. We are off 5 holidays per year, so your available working time is down to 15 days. We generously give you 14 days vacation per year which leaves only 1 day available for work and you're NOT going to take that day off!!!

————————

Good works are not a means of salvation because we are saved by grace through faith. We are saved only on the grounds of the death and resurrection of Jesus Christ.

But, our good works are an EVIDENCE of salvation; and if we fail to do all the good we can, to all the people we can, at any time we can, by any means we can, we will be condemned at the judgment bar of God.

CHRIST'S HANDS

During the war, a church in Strasburg, Germany, was totally destroyed; but a statue of Christ which stood by the altar was almost unharmed. Only the hands of the statue were missing. When the church was rebuilt, a famous sculptor offered to make new hands; but, after considering the matter, the members decided to let it stand as it was – without hands. "For," they said, "Christ has no hands but our hands to do His work on earth."

ONE DAUGHTER?

Several days in the hospital had not improved Elizabeth's disposition. She had no patience with nurses, doctors, or anyone else. A lady running a dust mop under her bed, trying to be friendly, started small talk.

"How many children do you have?" she asked.

That was the wrong question. On the previous day Elizabeth had been asleep, (much needed sleep) during both of my visits, so she was feeling lonely, unloved, & neglected.

"My only daughter lives in California!" was her sharp sarcastic response.

Her friend, Rudy, standing next to her bed, gasped, "Why, Elizabeth! What a dreadful thing to say! Here comes Betty now."

"Betty doesn't care about me. She just doesn't give a darn, so I don't consider her my daughter!"

As I entered the room, the dust-mop lady slipped past me, wearing a confused half grin. I urged Rudy to ignore the wee "pity-party" & help me unload my aching arms; a clean robe, a clean wig, a stack of mail, a sewing kit to repair her torn slipper, & a single pink rosebud in a pink vase.

"It's OK...don't fuss," I urged him. He looked so concerned.

My moment of disgust & hurt & annoyance passed quickly. So did my urge to toss her things on a chair & head for home. My Mom's rudeness was only part of the nasty attitude she often displayed toward me. It had become an UNFUNNY family joke that my sister & I recognized. She had never ever done anything wrong, & I had never ever done anything right. We had often prayed about it, & even laughed about it.

At that moment, the Lord seemed to remove the stabbing emotional pain & replaced it with an extra measure of gentle patience...a virtue I've never been able to claim as my own. A sense of sweet calmness poured over me, like warm oil, past my head, & down over my shoulders.

I tidied up Mom's bed, repaired her torn slipper, & then leaned over to share with her the cards & letters I'd brought from her apartment. Noise in the hall made it necessary to lean very close, so she could hear me. The cards were lovely, & she began to relax.

Inside a partially open drawer, I spotted the "Good News for Modern Man, New Testament and Psalms." In my hands, it fell open to Psalm 99 and Psalm 100. So many loving thoughts. Words of comfort & praises to the Lord.

"The Lord is King – He is mighty – Oh Lord, our God, You answer Your people – You are a God of forgiveness – You forgive us. – Give thanks to Him ..." I continued to read softly.

A tear falling on my hand, caused me to look up. Mom's eyes were full to the brim & overflowing.

"Sure don't know why I'm always so mean & nasty to you, when you truly are so good to me. Ask Jesus to forgive me & help me to be sweeter to you, and to everyone." She wept, & patted my hand.

I did, He did, and she truly was sweeter from then till she died, just a few months before her 100th Birthday.

CAN ORDINARY BE INTERESTING?

Bessie Graves called herself ordinary. She always had a poor self image. She was born fourth, in a poor family of seven children. Her Momma left home, taking the oldest, the youngest, & one not yet born, when Bessie was six. Bessie looked under the beds, thinking her Momma was hiding.

From then on, little Bessie felt left out, & even wondered if it was her fault Momma left in the middle of the night. Her drinking Daddy was the real cause, & Bessie lived with him, with two bossy sisters, & an older brother, Ray, whom she idolized, & followed like a shadow.

When Bessie was twelve, Ray asked her to go to a dance. She was thrilled & felt honored, till he started to "WOO" a girl who agreed to date him. How hurt & lost poor Bessie felt, to be left at the dance, with no way home. Her self-image plummeted.

Soon after that, Bessie was sent to live with an elderly couple, as their helper. They were cool & unaffectionate, but they taught her to be clean, polite, industrious, & faithful. She lived through life with no religious training. Following the FIRST BIG WAR, she lost Ray, who later had the questionable honor of becoming the first to jump off the Blue Water Bridge at Port Huron, after his horrible ordeal in WWI.

Bessie moved to Detroit to live with a married sister, who soon found her a job in a bakery. Her long, wavy red hair, lovely brown eyes, & shy nature attracted a blue-eyed blond fella' named Jack. Jack's family teased him & grew tired of the delicious cream puffs he bought nearly every day from that little bakery.

Bess & Jack were married in 1917, & lived in Detroit all their lives. Helen was born in 1918 & Betty in 1923. Bessie was an excellent cook & perfect housekeeper. Her search for love & acceptance was fueled by the praises she got at 12, when her skills at household chores were rewarded.

During the early years, Bessie was shy, reserved, quiet, easily offended, & a stay-at-home Mom, not attending PTA meetings or family gatherings; considered aloof by some.

Jack was one of 13 children in a busy, loving, noisy Roman Catholic family. Bessie never ever really felt included, but I see now, it was her reaction, not their actions, that caused her feelings of isolation.

Helen married Carl; they had one child, Beverly, & moved to California. Betty married Bob & they had three children, Nadene, Ron, & Linda. Those basics don't seem unusual, but Bessie again felt sad & rejected. Even though everyone tried to include her & kept trying to please her...nothing made her happy. Her tongue was sharp, her tears were frequent & her days were lonely & long.

When dear, sweet, whistling Jack died at 68, Bessie decided she hated her name. "Bessie is a cow's name. From now on I am Elizabeth!" she declared & never wavered.

After she accepted Jesus Christ as her Savior, she became THE NEW PERSON, *II Corinthians 5:17 – "Therefore if any man be in Christ, he is a new creature: old things are passed away; behold, all things are become new."

As the bible described; we all rejoiced with her and for her!

Later, while preparing her for surgery, the doctor & nurses told me Bessie wouldn't respond. When I called her Elizabeth, she grinned & opened her eyes. Her new feisty personality was emerging.

When she was 90, the doctor said "Elizabeth at your age, don't you expect the parts to wear out?"

"Yes, doctor, but the other foot is just as old, & it doesn't hurt," was her answer.

95

Bessie Elizabeth was the name we added to all of her insurance & other legal data. She was always a stylish dresser, kept her home immaculately clean, kept her finances in order & lived independently, till she was 96.

When a friend was robbed, walking down the street after church, Elizabeth asked me for an old purse. She would not explain till after we bought an old used one at a rummage sale. She then found an old wallet, some old keys that fit nothing, & some old letters addressed to OCCUPANT. As she assembled all those, she found a comb & some cleansing tissues, I was consumed with curiosity. She finally, grinning widely, explained, "If anyone steals MY purse, they're getting trash. My money & my house keys are in a tiny bag inside my pocket, so there!" Clever lady.

One day Elizabeth asked us to take her to visit several nursing homes. She chose one, put her name on their waiting list, & said, "No one will ever put me in a nursing home. When I'm ready I will decide when & where!" She did.

Meanwhile, on the back or bottom of every item she owned, she wrote the date purchased, or received as a gift, from whom, or the price, and ...the person who should receive it, when she no longer needed it. Every chair & pillowcase had a label. She was ready to move whenever the time came.

One day she said, "I'm ready, but I'll pay a month's rent here. It's due tomorrow." "Are you afraid you won't like it & want to move back here?" I asked.

"NO—but it took me a lifetime to collect all these lovely things, & I don't want them to go to the wrong person or place," she declared. Now we were seeing a happier, more decisive person daily.

In the new surroundings Elizabeth's personality bloomed & sweetened. She had become more alert, outgoing, wise & humorous at 96.

One day I called her & asked, "Hi! Honey, watcha' doin'?" She answered, "I'm memorizing the parts of a horse from the new book Helen sent me." Since her early days on a farm, she had loved horses, & Helen was wise to send her the big book.

I wondered why she'd memorize...but...I rejoiced at her new project.

The staff warned Elizabeth not to leave money around, as it sometimes had a way of disappearing. When someone stole her $5.00 bill, she devised a plan. That same lovely book about horses had one $5.00 bill on page 8, another one on page 31, another one on page 18 and one more on page 96. It took me a moment to discover her strategy. Her birthday was August 31, 1896. Now she had her money handy as needed, but not available to "stealers." Who, besides Elizabeth, would care about her horse book?

Just before Elizabeth's 99th birthday, Bob decided to drive to Montana to spend his vacation with our son, Ron. "Oh no! must you leave two days before Mom's big birthday bash?" I asked him. Bob didn't want to be driving on the Labor Day weekend, so he felt he must leave on August 30th. "She'll have a fit. You're so special to her!" I urged.

"Can't you fool her about the date? You've got two weeks to steal her calendar," was Bob's solution to that big dilemma.

So, I broke the hook that hung her calendar, took it home to "fix it", & just kept forgetting to return it. Lying felt evil.

On the 29th we took a huge meal, with all her favorites, to the dining room at her place. Roast beef with carrots & baby onions, creamy mashed potatoes, homemade coleslaw, & strawberries to slosh over her angel food birthday cake. Eleven candles, one for every nine years, made her laugh. Big hit!

Bob told Mom that night about his trip to visit Ron; she wished him well & promised to pray for him.

After we all left, as the nurses prepared her for bed, she told them, "Those kids went to a lotta' fuss for my birthday. They think they fooled me—&— I LET them think so. It makes them happy—I hope Bob has a safe trip. I wonder when he'll return." After more preparation, she added, "When Betty puts my calendar back up; maybe she'll tell me why Bob left early. G'nite, dear."

When our granddaughter, Christine, & I drove to Florida, my Mom Elizabeth had become very deaf & her sight was diminishing rapidly. Bob agreed to visit her briefly every other day during our absence. He asked, "How on earth will I answer the thousand questions she asks every time?" He then reminded me of the time I visited & she asked, "How's Bob? What's he doing today?" The next day Bob was asked, "How's Betty? What's she doing today?" When we both told her we didn't know what the other one was doing, her quick question was, "What are you two fighting about? Why doncha' know what he is doin'?" I quickly told her, "Honey, that's what keeps us FROM fighting! We each do our own thing, & meet every evening for supper! OK?"

After we left for Florida, the second time Bob visited Elizabeth, she asked him, "Where's Betty? She hasn't been here for years!" He tried to tell her about the trip to Florida Christine & I were taking. She could not hear. Bob has had allergies for years, so, as he kept blowing his nose, she assumed, "Oh, Betty has a cold too. Stay away from me; I don't want your germs!" She waved & shoved him out the door. Bob chose not to visit for three more days, hoping that she would still believe that he had a cold.

When he went to see her several days later, the scene was an instant replay—her questions—Bob's nose blowing...her assumption—& then he left again feeling guilty. BUT what could he do? He couldn't make her hear him. He tried to write a note & she couldn't see it. Oh woe!

Christine & I returned about 11 p.m. twelve days later. Bob hugged us & said, "Go see your Mom! She thinks you're dying from a cold. She asks me what the doctor sez' boutcha'!"

Early the next day I used a felt pen to write a note with letters five inches high, to tell her about our trip to see Christine's other gramma in Florida.

Elizabeth shouted, "Oh, I'm glad you had a good time—BUT you should've told Bob where you were. He was sick with worry about you. Every time he came to see me he cried."

It wasn't easy to explain the situation to her. It took stacks of paper & felt pens. She finally GOT IT.

A few months before her 100th birthday, Elizabeth peacefully went to be with her good friend, Jesus.

We didn't expect a very large turnout at her funeral. Not many friends & family members are still alive by that age. But employees from her "new" home & many other folks appeared. Our new Pastor spoke graciously of Elizabeth's new life in Christ, & then he invited everyone to our home afterwards! As I turned to see that large group of people, my heart pounded. We had planned to take the dozen family members who came, to a local eatery. My grandchildren & I exchanged frantic glances. That cake I baked last night wouldn't go far. We left for the cemetery, wondering what we would feed all those people.

At the cemetery, we waited & waited, & waited, & waited for the Pastor. He was new to town, so perhaps he got lost. Finally, a family friend, Pastor Relinda Mushatt offered her assistance. "Oh yes! Please, Please!" I gratefully accepted.

Pastor Mushatt did a lovely, unplanned memorial service & again invited everyone to our home. WOW! I was shocked! Could we stop for takeouts?

My grandkids & I didn't know that members of that Pastor's congregation were alerted to prepare & bring large containers of coleslaw, potatoes, chicken, etc. to serve to our guests. As dozens of cars arrived, we were all stunned. We were amazed to see the food & the folks come in simultaneously!

Our own Pastor moaned & apologized for getting lost, & not ever finding the right cemetery. But we never stopped teasing him for getting back to our house in time for lunch. Elizabeth would have laughed.

We also have never stopped thanking the Lord, for our other loving Pastor's presence & for her congregation's willingness to serve & share.

In a moment of reminiscing & prayer recently, Pastor Mushatt thanked God that He had prompted her to slip her little black book in her purse the day of my Mom's funeral. None of us had expected our Pastor to get lost, but God knew & prepared her for it. "We never stop thanking You, Father, You did it again!"

WHAT MAKES PEOPLE WORRY?

Dy'a ever wonder what that funny attraction is that some folks call "chemical?" When we meet certain people we like them immediately (or some folks we just don't like) but, I admit it is extremely unusual to feel that true love about the lady who will become your Mother-in-law in two years. Let me tell you about her.

Bob & I married in 1943. We lived in Texas about four years while he was in the army in WWII, then we returned to Detroit. Those first years we moved many times. Bob's Mom & Dad visited often, as did my folks & all our sisters & brothers. Then, in 1956 when we had moved to Saginaw, Bob's Mom came to live with us. She called me her "Daughter-in-love." Our kids adored her. We became "Best friends."

In many families, the late night fone call sez, "We've had Mom long enough! It's your turn!" In our family, Bob's brothers & sisters would call & say, "You've had Mom long enough. It's our turn!" So, of course, she'd go to visit her other four kids, all over the country. But, she always called this her home.

The only time Gram Hazel & I ever had a fight (what a joke) was the morning I put dirty clothes from our three children, Bob, & me...(but none from Gram) in the washing machine in the basement. I ran up to the second floor to ask her why. She tipped her head to one side & shyly answered, "You have so much to do, and I can wash my own things & save you the trouble."

First I stamped my foot jokingly & said, "That is a pile of rubbish...along side the dirty clothes. The biggest trouble is...you making me come up two flights of steps to get them! No more of that nonsense, right?"

I hugged & kissed her & said, "Instead of wasting your time washing your clothes that my washer can do quicker & easier...why not just come down & set the table for lunch? OK?" We both laughed.

Gram Hazel was probably the most loving, gentle, Christ-like person I've ever met. One morning she looked very tired. "Why do you look like you've been up all night? Are you ill?" I asked.

"No, dear. I...uh...I...spent most of the night apologizing to God," she had her head down.

"What on earth do YOU have to apologize to God for? I can't picture you ever offending or disobeying HIM!" I said in a high pitched voice.

"Well, every night, just after I say my prayers, I listen to that radio station, where "Bill somebody" talks about the Bible & says comforting wise things that help me fall asleep. He said that when we grumble & complain it shows that we criticize God's decisions...AND...when we worry we INSULT Him. Soooo, I spent the rest of the night apologizing to God," she said with tears streaming down her cheeks.

We hugged & prayed together; to thank God that Jesus forgives all our sins, even our complaining & all our worrying. She noted that worry should be on the same list as murder & gossip. She asked me to remind her to break that bad habit, but I reminded her God will help her to break it & forgive her anyway.

Several days later, Gram told us that worry is like a rocking chair. It keeps you busy, but you don't get any where.

One day, as I stood at the sink, I remarked, "When Linda climbs so high on that play bar it scares me!"

Gram Hazel smiled & advised, "Either go & take her down, or look the other way...It doesn't help to worry, dear."

I recently read these thoughts & hope they can be helpful to someone who battles WORRY.

> Worry is interest paid in advance on something you may never own.

People would worry less about what others think of them if they only realized how seldom they do.

> Worry gives a small thing a big shadow. It is simply the misuse of the creative imagination God has placed within each of us. Many people believe their doubts and doubt their beliefs. So follow the old saying: "feed your faith, and watch your doubts starve to death." Too much analysis always leads to paralysis. Instead, take your fear and worry to the Lord, "Casting all your

care upon Him; for He careth for you" (1 Pet. 5:7).

Worry is a route that leads from somewhere to nowhere. Never let it direct your life.

In a "different" version of the bible, Philippians 4:6-7 says, "Instead of worrying, pray. Let petitions & praises shape your worries into prayers, letting God know your concerns. Before you know it, a sense of God's wholeness, everything coming together for good, will come & settle you down."

Makes good sense to me!

RANDOM THOUGHTS OF A DINOSAUER

It's awkward to shift gears in my thinking. At times I dig in my heels & refuse. I'm not so sure that all the stuff thrust upon us as PROGRESS, really is. As I RE...LAX on my front porch I wonder if today's progress will bring the pleasures I remember.

Now I reflect on:

I've heard that the world could literally "fall apart at the seams" when ladies my age die off...cuz...so few under 50, choose to sew. If they tried, they just might enjoy it, & even learn it can be profitable!

I've heard that today's younger people are truly brilliant about technology. BUT many of them can't make a sandwich & some can't make their bed. SAD. Priorities?

I've recently read that those under 25 show a reviving interest in the art of volunteering. They're discovering the true joy of helping others, & doing worthwhile projects, without a paycheck. Most of their parents show no interest at all. What will happen to those fine, helpful organizations like Red Cross, Scouting, museums, libraries, & hospital gift shops...till the 14 thru 24 year olds take over?

Someone explained to me why underwear, & slacks & Pjs turn wrong side out (or their pockets protrude) in the washer, but, I'm still puzzled. Do you understand it?

Wish I'd get as many envelopes from folks I know, as I get from folks I don't know, & don't even want to know.

It's sad to see NAMES written in all small letters. Capital letters denote respect, but then, how much respect do we express today?

Is there any sound more universally enjoyed than the giggles of a wee child?

What is the unwritten (or written) law that dictates which plants we nurture & transplant, as valuable for gardens,...and which ones (that grow happily in most places under most conditions) should be dug up & discarded as weeds? Has anyone ever considered switching the categories? Just think how simple life would be, if we adults loved dandelions as much as kids do. They made lovely necklaces & gifts when we were about 4.

Most of us are urged to recycle. I'm sad to see so much destruction of tile countertops & bathrooms, just for new color scheme, & to be updated. Why are those folks not trained & urged to recycle? Couldn't some of those old bath tubs be used in the homes of poor folks with a broken or scarred tub? Or, is that just too old fashioned to consider?

The United States is called an infant, compared to those ancient civilizations & countries who have buildings thousands of years old. As we tear down our old buildings, & build parking lots & drug stores, will we ever have any lovely old treasures to admire? I sure hope so.

It recently was said, that knee-mail is still better than Email. God probly' agrees. It may please many folks to read their Email each day...I personally find it COLD and impersonal. A friend recently said, "I'd rather have a paper letter that I can re-read, & a paper photo that I can frame & look at again & again". By the way, that friend is only 22.

Does anyone remember pulley clotheslines? Guess it was a big-city thing. I vividly remember sitting on the back porch of our second floor flat in Detroit, watching my Mother hang mountains of freshly washed wet clothes. That strange squeaky line came to the porch; she securely fastened each towel, sheet, and our dresses on it, and then, she pulled & tugged on that crazy rope clothesline till it returned to the barn. It seemed to be a mile away to us children; it may have been about 30 feet. BUT my Daddy's trousers were so high above the ground, that we couldn't reach them, when we jumped as high as we could. They were all hand washed in a big tub, hand rinsed to remove all of the soap, hand wrung out, & Oh!...They smelled so good when Mom took them off that strange pulley clothesline. I never did quite figure out how it worked, but, I'll never forget the sheets hanging high over our heads halfway between the house & the barn.

Folks now order waffles at a coffee shop & think they're good. That's only because they never had one that the "Waffle man" usta' make in his big truck & serve to us, for a nickel on the side streets of Detroit! We could smell that luscious fragrance, & hear that strange melodic sound from a block away. "Waffles, WAA'fuls, WAA'fuls, Comandgetem!" All the while he was pouring that magic creamy stuff on that ugly black, steaming hot waffle iron. Fluffy white powdered sugar was sprinkled on top. They were almost too hot to eat. When we smiled & giggled, the Waffleman would say, "I'll put some ice cream on if you don't tell anybody!" We told everyone! My heart races to think of them.

You may think your Gramma was the best bread maker in the world...NO...mine was. She had a specialty that was the best food ever invented. She had ten adult children, plus their spouses & grandkids, who all just dropped in to eat any day, any time. So, she spent her life baking bread, cookies, cakes & pies. Each time I entered the front door, the fragrances wafting on the breeze warned me of the REAL butter sizzling all around the edges of her big black iron skillet. She kissed me on the forehead, & continued the lovely ritual that only she could do. I can still hear Gram's strong hands slapping the big patty of raw bread dough, then, dropping it gently into those golden bubbles of butter. It quickly became a lovely white cloud, (smelled amazing) incased in a crispy, crunchy golden brown coating that cannot be described, or duplicated. Ohh! WOW!

Does anyone remember a "Sheeny?" I cannot find the word in dictionaries, so I'm not sure of the correct spelling. I was told it was an Ethnic word. In Detroit, there were dozens of nationalities in most neighborhoods, so it may have been known there, if not other places. Our Sheeny was the forerunner of modern rummage sales & garage sales ... on wheels.

He was always welcomed by kids & adults alike. We eagerly searched through the treasures packed tightly in & on his magic wagon. Many items may have been bought, for a penny or two, from his regular customers on the blocks before he reached our block. That was about 1932.

He could be heard coming down the alley several blocks away, as he half shouted & half sang his deep throated melodic chant, "Sheeny, Sheeny, your Sheeny is here. Sheeny, Sheeny, here comes your Sheeny!" Over & over, he announced his arrival, in his thick, charming, upbeat, heavy accent. LOUD.

We all suspected it was more than just pennies that kept him at his chosen profession. He surely loved the way folks of all ages, & all colors, & all professions, greeted him with all kinds of homemade treats. Cookies, breads, & soups & pies awaited him. His grin was contagious. His wagon was stuffed so full he had items pinned & nailed into place & hanging all over the outside of his wagon too. No one ever stole from him. He called everyone friend...not customers...all friends.

At first the Sheeny had a knobby-kneed old horse drawing his wagon. Later, the whole neighborhood rejoiced when he drove up in a used...very used...old truck. It was packed just as full as his old wagon, but just a bit neater looking.

Some of the items we bought from him for a penny (or two or three) are now priceless treasures on a bureau or on a fireplace mantel. I inherited from my Mom, the spatula she bought from the Sheeny for two cents. I use it daily. We wonder whatever happened to the shoehorn & the brass letter-opener that he bought from us, for two pennies each.

Our Daddy bought a brand new robin-egg blue Star car in the late 1920's, for about $660.00. It had isinglass window curtains, (but they really were windows). We spent many happy, giggling hours, snapping them on & off, for our brand new air-conditioning. Daddy felt ten inches taller when he drove it.

In 2001 while visiting friends in CA we enjoyed a display of old cars. No one had ever believed me when I told them about the price & color of Daddy's Star car, till they saw one there, priced at $695 from

1926...Daddy musta' got a bargain.

Another vivid memory was the fun my sister & I had climbing in & out of our uncle's Model A Ford. Climb up onto the back wheel, over the fender & then slide down into the rumble seat. We hated rainy days. They prevented our exciting ride in the RUMBLE SEAT.

Life is hard by the yard; it's a cinch by the inch.

Most of us know a perfectionist. I gave each of my sewing class pupils a copy of an old 'saying' & had them say it together in unison: "The pursuit of excellence is gratifying & healthy. The pursuit of perfection is frustrating & neurotic...as well as the terrible waste of time & energy, & even friendships."
If they wanted perfection they should seek another teacher. I would always expect excellence, so they'd be proud of their results. Years later one of those early pupils told me that the phrase on paper, was posted in her kitchen & blessed her for years. We never know how far the ripples go...do we?
So, let's not teach our kids that "Practice makes perfect"...It might make excellence, but perfect is the wrong goal. Only Jesus is perfect. It's wise to work hard to be like HIM, but we can never be perfect.

Your Dreams may be odd & even silly, but they can't be as silly as mine.
Our car was packed with kids & luggage as we started on a trip.
After driving about two hours, my husband announced, "Can you believe it...we're out of gas. We'll hafta' go home & get some more."
So, we did.

Expecting a large group of guests, for dinner, I cooked all day. As the time approached, I decided to get dishes out to set the table. My cupboard was about 40 feet long, floor to ceiling. As I opened every door & drawer, I kept finding kettles & buckets & glass jars, but no dishes...none .... The door bell rang; my guests arrived, all carrying their own dishes, which all matched. I wasn't even surprised, just served the meal & everyone put their dishes in their pockets to go home. That wasn't just a Dream it seemed like a nightmare!

————————

There are so many varieties of shells...& millions of each variety. BUT...I must remember that a few of just the right ones are far more inspiring & beautiful than a big pile of others. So it is with friends. A few of just the right ones make us happier than dozens of others.

When I asked my Grampa, "Were you born in France or Belgium?" He curtly answered, "yes," with a grin. He taught my Irish Gramma (Mary Ann Kilroy) how to make all of those "ethnic" dishes, including head-cheese. She taught me lots of them, but I never even wanted to know that one. I've never ever met another man named Simeon Valentine Formaz. Gramma & Grampa had 13 children, but there were no more to carry on that last name. Their sons all had daughters, and their daughters had sons. But, the Formaz name seems to have ended.

Lotsa' people love sauerkraut.
Lotsa' people hate sauerkraut.
How many people have ever made sauerkraut? My Daddy did. I watched, & even helped a little...and...we called it fun.
The crock it was made in was big enough for us kids to hide in when we were six & eight years old.
The cabbage was partly throw-away- heads that a local farmer felt were not good enough to sell at his roadside market. Since my Daddy brought home only $10.00 for two week's pay (including overtime), he worked feverishly at his wee garden & never quit seeking true bargains.
That garden was the major part of our back yard. It may have been about thirty by twenty feet. Daddy tried to grow everything that would grow in Michigan. But, he knew that his farmer friend grew cabbages by the zillions & would save the scrubby ones for Daddy. He usually got a bushel full.
Over the top of that huge crock, Daddy placed the grater. To us it looked sorta' like an ironing board (without the legs). It had a square flat boxy thing with very sharp wide blades in it. The cabbage sat on it & was sliced as that box was pushed back & forth.
A layer of cabbage, a layer of salt (a big handful) a layer of cabbage, a handful of salt, a layer of cabbage, etc. Then, a large clean white sheet of canvas or lineny fabric covered it all. Next, Daddy placed a circle of wood with a hole in it, to lift it out. On top of all, he placed a very large heavy rock. Last of all Daddy wrote on the calendar "Kraut day," & we all sighed in relief.
No one touched it for awhile. I was too young to remember if it was

a week or longer. Then, EVERY day after work we'd all go out, lift the rock, the board & the "hood" of cloth. We'd take a wee bite & announce, "Its still cabbage".

Then, one day, we'd taste it & scream, "Its KRAUT!" Guess what we'd have for supper that nite, & once a week from then on, till the crock was empty & ready for hide & seek.

THE FIRST NIGHT BEFORE CHRISTMAS

T'was the night before Christmas
They arrived in that town,
The inns were all full,
No place to lie down.
> Out back was a stable;
> It had clean straw and hay
> Where the animals were resting
> At the close of the day.
There was room in the stable
To lie down for to rest,
So Mary and Joseph
Praised God and felt blessed.
> In the clean straw of the stable,
> In the scent of fresh mown hay,
> Baby Jesus was born
> And in the manger He lay.
The animals softly snorted with glee
As they watched with joyous delight.
They know this child was very special
That was born on this very night.
> Out on the rolling hills
> In the chilly nighttime air,
> Shepherds watched their sleeping flocks
> While they spoke to God in prayer.
Then out of nowhere sweet music came
And a glorious brightness of light
That surrounded God's holy angel
To shatter their quiet night.
> "Do not be afraid" the angel said,
> "I bring you good news for all men.
> In the city of David, a child is born,

107

A Saviour for you" the angel told them.
"This is a sign, He lies in a manger
In swaddling clothes, the Christ child lay.
Go find Him and worship this holy one
As you kneel in the straw and pray."

    Then appeared a great host of angels
    Filling the sky with heavenly praise,
    Saying "Glory to God in the highest
    And on earth peace for all of man's days."

The shepherds were filled with wonder;
This child is one they must see
And so to Bethlehem they hurried
To see the fulfillment of prophesy.

    They found the appointed stable.
    In the manger, the holy child lay.
    Just as the angel had told them
    And they shared that message that day.

This is the long promised messiah
In the role as a carpenter's son.
No castles or robes of adornment
To begin a reign yet to come.

    "Now you have heard the true story
    Of the glory at the Saviour's birth.
    We celebrate this birth every Christmas
    And peace to men on earth."

Luke 2:4-20   **Vernice L. Darland**

WE CAN'T AFFORD A PORCH

Having moved 21 times during our first 20 years of marriage, it felt great to finally be "at home" in our very own new house...&...it really was a brand new house. So, there were many things that needed attention.

The builder repaired oodles of problems, those that usually surface in a new building. The oven wasn't connected, electrical switches had problems, (minor but annoying), the dishwasher washed the dishes, but the water couldn't leave...someone goofed. We had lotsa' giggles & snickers & even a few tears, but finally everything seemed to be just great.

A picnic, in the back yard, through the lovely sliding glass doors off the dining room, was planned with anticipation. Lotsa' good food, several visitors, lovely day, lotsa' sunshine...OOPS! We had not tried to sit out there before...BIG problem! We had not even thought about the very white, very shiny siding on the entire house, and the large white square of concrete; very white concrete.

We all squinted a bit, as we arranged our luscious food on the big picnic table. BUT, by the time we were all seated, we couldn't open our eyes to even see each other. The sun felt lovely & warm, but the reflection was truly unbearable. We moved the table off the porch, (the big white slab) onto the grass, but it was still dazzling.

We opted to bring all that yummy food into the dining room to eat. Big disappointment.

The next day we tried to locate someone to build a roof over a screened-in porch. The cost of materials was just the tip of the proverbial iceberg. Labor of a professional carpenter would be truly out of our financial reach. We just cannot afford to build a real porch. "Let's face it, that will hafta' wait till next year, unless we have a rich uncle we've never met," was Bob's decision. The three kids pouted & left the room

Seventeen year old, Nadene was more upset than we knew at the time. Asking around at church, she learned (from her girlfriend's Dad) of a retired carpenter who just might be available. His name was Claude.

It took no trouble to find Claude, & his schedule was open. He stopped by, calmly measured the concrete slab as he hummed & whistled. We nervously watched & waited till he dropped off a list of "stuff to buy," scribbled on the back of an old wrinkled envelope from his back pocket. He left saying, "G'bye, call me when you get the "stuff."

When hubby Bob came in from work, his first question was, "How much will he charge to build it?" We all shrugged & suggested he call Claude to find out. He was reluctant to call, & asked if I'd call him. "Naw, I think that's up to you," I said cowardly. We put the idea on the back burner.

The next week, the kids yelled, "Hey! Look what Daddy's got...a bunch of wood & stuff!" They helped unload it all & piled it in the garage. I wondered, but said nothing.

After another week passed Nadene asked, "Daddy, do you want me to call Claude?" "No, Honey, I will." Later that evening, Bob said, "Claude's coming to start the porch tomorrow."

"Oh! WOW! Did he say how much he will charge us?" I asked.

"Welllll...no...not really. He just said we could afford it." Bob hesitated & then added, "I'm not sure what that means, but, I couldn't even get him to say what time tomorrow. Strange fella'."

At seven a.m., before everyone was dressed & fed, we heard faint noises in the back yard. Claude unloaded his big assortment of tools, and, an odd looking large, yellow, plastic cushion, that he placed against the wall, next to the concrete slab. HMMM...wonder what that's for.

He greeted us with his gentle demeanor, (his head dropped to one side), & wide grin, but said only, "G'mornin!" He winked at little Linda. No one said another word; everyone just ran to carry all of the "wood stuff" from the garage to the slab.

While I cleaned up the breakfast mess, I heard normal sounds of sawing & hammering. Then it got very quiet. As I peaked out the back, I saw Claude seated on that mysterious yellow cushion, leaned up against the base of the house, surrounded by four year old Linda, 12 year old Ronny, 17 year old Nadene, and three neighbor kids. They were all chewing big wads of bubble gum, & trying to whistle (with Claude) to the tune of "Whistle While You Work." And...giggling like crazy. It was 10 AM.

I assumed that was break time, but was shocked to learn that Claude had gone home. Three more days, the exact same schedule, but different songs, left me puzzled.

When Bob & I went out to survey the progress, we were not expecting what we found. The roof, the ceiling, & posts on eight locations were expertly completed. A little later, Claude stopped by & handed us a very neatly written paper...his bill...& then I asked him why eight posts? Bob opened the bill. It was $40 due. Claude quietly grinned & answered me, "For the doorway, of course." We hadn't even considered the need for a door.

Bob protested, "Claude, we truly appreciate all you've done, so professionally, but it surely is worth more than $40 dollars!"

"Well, I had fun with the kids, & wasn't busy at all this week, so, that's plenty. Call me when you're ready to put the screens up. G'bye." He left smiling, with the big yellow cushion under his arm.

On Bob's next day off, he spent the entire day (just sneaking a quick lunch break) with tape measure & yard sticks, measuring every angle on the porch.

"If it took you all day to measure it, Honey, how long will it take to build all the screens?" I asked. Bob grinned, "Call Claude." I did.

Claude told us exactly what to buy. He didn't even need to measure it again. He remembered. He came four more days...the exact same schedule as before...& charged another $40. I did send a big batch of oatmeal cookies & a loaf of homemade bread home with him though. He just smiled & hugged the kids, as he carted off his yellow cushion.

That was 51 years ago. The porch is still strong & straight & secure, & has had several coats of paint. Dear old Claude would be happy to know of all the blessings he & his lovely porch brought to our whole family, even the grandchildren of those kids he taught to whistle.

TIPS FOR WRITING THANK –YOU NOTES

We are always surprised when we hear grown people shrug off thank-you notes. No, it doesn't matter if Grandma was sitting with you as you opened the gift from her; you still owe her a formal thank-you note. An email won't do either. And yes, even if you have horrible hand-writing, you must still sit down and hand-write a card to each person who was kind enough to give you a gift this season.

With all of that said, we do understand that the thought of writing thank-you cards can be daunting, especially if you received a lot of gifts. Here are simple tips that will help you organize yourself so that you get yours done before the week is out, and without breaking a sweat.

1. Keep a list. It sounds simple, but it's amazing how often this little thing is overlooked. Keep a pad and pencil handy as you and your family open gifts. Document who got what from whom; then when it comes time to write your thank-you notes, there won't be any confusion.
2. Grab a pen and paper. Refrain from sending an email. Handwritten notes feel special, almost like the person is there with you. ...Or just post cards will do fine. My kids tease me cuz I recycle & make post-cards.
3. Keep it short. Your message doesn't need to be long and eloquent – my cards are small, with room for only three or four sentences. By sticking to a few lines, you keep the focus on your thank-you and on the other person's kindness.

These tips are ideas from several sources. Can't remember who or when.

**Serving the Lord
and having fun!**

112

1939

The Piano

1996

The Porch

Our great granddaughter said, "Gram, don't ever sell this home, it's truly the nicest home ever!" We agree.

Bob's photo wall.

Anza Borrego Desert, CA.
1999 B.C. (Before Cell 'fones)

DISAGREEMENT

I read that when Mrs. Billy Graham was asked if she & her husband ever disagree, her answer was simple. "If two people agree on everything...one of them is unnecessary."

Although Bob & I did not plan it, we somehow agreed to learn to disagree agreeably...usually...most of the time, at least.

However, one Saturday night, Bob arrived home & announced excitedly, "Hey, Hon! Look, I just bought a garage door opener...It was on sale...a real bargain!"

"Oh no, I thought we discussed all large things...there's only enough money to pay our Consumers bill that's due Monday. We just hafta' take it back, & wait till next month. Sorry, Honey," I moaned, trying to look understanding.

"Rod & I are gonna' install it tomorrow, just in time. It's s'posta' get cold & rainy next week." He sounded like he hadn't even heard my cautious wisdom.

"No, Bob, didn't you hear me? We cannot keep it. The Consumers bill will need every penny, or they'll turn our lights off!" I warned again.

"Relax, Sweetie, it will be OK!" Bob said calmly. Nothing annoyed me more than his calm assurances, when I was certain we faced a threatening tragedy. At bed time I said, "Oh well, you'll be sitting in the dark & hungry too...when they turn off the lights & gas," I added, with a big frown. He hugged me. "I promise, we'll be fine," again annoyingly serene. How could he be so sure, I wondered.

Sunday they installed the garage door opener, in the sunshine. Bob & Rod laughed & laughed, as they ran the crazy thing up & down. I asked if they might wear it out. Bob hugged me again, grinning, like a victorious prize fighter. "It'll be OK," he assured me again.

As he drove out on Monday, Bob couldn't control the urge to run that garage door up & down another 97 times, in the rain.

That day Gram Hazel had a sore throat, & when her fever increased, the doctor urged me to bring her in. Our three children attended three different schools, so, it took quite a trip to pick them all up (in the pouring rain) & take Gram to the doctor's office. It rained harder.

On the way home, we needed to stop at the store for milk, eggs & Gram's medicines. All this in the icy rain, which was becoming sleet. It was very slippery!

As we drove into the icy driveway, I firmly pushed the button, & the garage door opened with elegant obedience & a rumbling fan-fare.

WOW! The three kids laughed & clapped. Gram & I just grinned.

Before I even removed my coat, I rushed to the telephone & dialed Bob's office number.

"Oh! Mrs. Sharrer, I dare not put a call through to Mr. Sharrer. He's in a big important meeting with the BIG BOYS...the owners from Detroit. I just CAN"T!" his secretary declared emphatically.

I convinced her I would take the blame. "Just hold the 'fone up to his ear & I will do the rest," I insisted. I heard the door open as she entered, & quietly said Bob's name. I said very quickly, "I am sooooooo glad we have a garage door opener!" & I hung up.

As Bob arrived home, late that evening, his smile was wide, & his hug was the warmest one I ever remember. I cannot remember how we paid that Consumers bill, but it did get paid.

THE NOTE

One Saturday many years ago, my husband was in a meeting with out-of-town business men, when I called his office. He could not be interrupted. His secretary agreed to write my message carefully & hand it to him, as he left the meeting. The note said:

"My Father is very ill, so the three children & I are taking a Greyhound Bus to Detroit. We will return Sunday evening. The car will be parked on Baum St. near the bus station. Love, Betty & the kids."

Later that evening, when Bob left his office, he went to his familiar parking lot. After searching for 20 minutes, he called me. No answer. Then he called the Police Dept. to report his car stolen. He & the police, driving all over Saginaw, found the car near the bus station. On Baum St.

At home, another note told him of my dad's illness & we'd be home Sunday. My dad was in the hospital, so I didn't call Bob from Detroit. I felt he would understand from the two notes I had left for him. When we returned, we wondered why he was upset. His secretary insisted she had told him. Bob vowed he was too young to forget such a vital message.

The next day as I put soiled sox & shirts in the washer, I found THE note in his shirt pocket.

Poor Bob...his red face & silly grin proved he "got the message," even though it took two notes and a policeman to do it.

MANY NOTES

As the manager of a very large retail store, Bob's long hours & goofy schedules made his return home unpredictable. After so many meals away from home, he looked forward to home cooking, so, he decided to tell me each morning the time he expected to get home "give or take an hour," so I could have his meals ready.

At first there were ordinary slips of paper with a few numbers & very few words. Soon they became more clever, creative, often silly, but usually fun.

One morning, he had obviously searched all over the house to find about 30 safety pins, closed them & arranged them to form a large 6.

Another morning his little note had a big arrow on it pointing to another identical note on the floor,...five in all...pointing to the TV, in the living room. The kids & I were giggling when we found where he had drawn a large 6:30 in the dust, on the top of the T.V.

I later laughed & admitted his message had a double meaning.

After a week of normal notes, one morning he had emptied the silverware drawer, to line up many spoons to form a big 7.

Another two weeks of just notes, & then a tiny note said, "Fluffy is joining us for dinner tonite. She prefers: bird, fish, or a mouse...about 6:30."

We wondered if the cat knew she was invited.

One morning Bob had taken several sox from his drawer & formed a large question mark?...all with sox. The kids giggled hysterically, & gave him extra hugs when he finally arrived at 8:30.

Bob's silliness was always true fun, & unexpected. We loved it...and him.

That's one more reason why our marriage lasted nearly 70 years!

THE RIFLE

No, I'm not talking about a gun. Perhaps you've never heard of the Rifle River in mid-Michigan, but it has interesting memories for me.

Let's start at the beginning. The Cornells had three kids, & so did we. When the Cornells suggested a canoe trip, I had mixed emotions.

Bob & I had often rented canoes as teens in a calm lake area near Detroit. It was just the two of us, madly in love, & too young to even consider danger. Where, when, & HOW do you do it on a wild river with six kids? The Cornells had done it before & had all the answers;

they thought.

I have no idea what day or date, but I vividly remember those plastic water-proof boxes that held our lunches.

The two husbands drove about 15 miles to rent the canoes, & already I was confused. I can still see those three canoes on top of the car. We were divided into three groups, & that gave me cold chills. I don't remember how we got into the canoes, nor how we got home, but...that canoe ride in between, I will never forget.

Just getting the five of us ready so early in the morning was the first challenge.

Lovely bright sunshine; lotsa' jackets, lotsa' hats with visors, lotsa' sunglasses & sunscreen, lotsa' plastic shoe box lunches, lotsa' giggles & squeals & screams, as our sons tormented our daughters.

Lush, verdant green scenery was beautiful. The first few miles were pleasant, but it soon became rockier; more curves, larger trees & wilder, wavy water. Giggles & gasps increased as the wind & waves increased. All of a sudden, the gasps turned to screams as rain fell like an upturned bucket.

Linda shouted, "Mamma, where do birds go when it rains?" I was more interested in where canoers go when it rains.

The rain stopped as abruptly as it had started. We all burst out laughing. How long will it take for drippy wet hair & wet shirts to dry? The hot sun felt good. Wet trees sparkled. The six kids sang camp songs & laughed, as they messed up the words. More rocks to avoid, more wild water. We careened around sharp curves, trying to miss the tops of partially submerged tree stumps & low hanging branches. One of the boys yelled, "WOW, this is funner than I thought it was!" His sister shouted, "Duck your head, silly!"

And then, another shower. Quick, short & unannounced, like the first one. Then a third...and...the men declared, "Let's stop for lunch." Someone said, "Daddy, it's only 10:30."

After we found a place to put-in, I was shocked to see the Cornells overturn the three canoes & suspend them on sturdy young trees & branches. It was odd to see the ten of us standing UNDER the canoes trying to unwrap & eat our lunches, without stepping in those plastic boxes.

I've often heard the sound of "rain on the roof." But it was a novelty to hear "rain on canoe bottoms." The third shower lasted longer than the first two, & we shivered, in our wet clothes.

We rejoiced briefly to be out of the intense rain & giggled at the efforts to eat standing up. But, then, we began to realize that a regiment of mosquitos had found our dry warm spot too. They buzzed so loud it sounded unreal; like one of those wonky movies with bumble-bees ten foot tall. We swatted, slapped, & yelled, as if they should obey us. Futile. Comical now, but not then.

Our twelve mile canoe trip on the Rifle River seemed doomed, till someone shouted, "Hey, the sun's out. Let's try again!" We all kept scratching, as the canoes were up-turned & all the wet gear was assembled. Bob's camera fell into the river & the plastic boxes had to be rescued several times, but we resumed our adventure.

The hot sun felt great & gave us new hope. But,...you've guessed it; the next rain was not just a playful shower. The drenching downpour had a totally different attitude & sound. We searched for a safe haven to put-in. Enough already!

We found a welcome clearing near a small hill. The two men began making plans to walk the two or three miles to get our cars & rescue the rest of us. We dreaded the idea of our daddies sloshing in the muddy woods in the rain storm, with lightening & thunder. But, sitting on wet logs or standing around in the torrential mess didn't seem too attractive either. The men fastened their wet jackets, as they tried to choose the right path through that ominous wilderness.

Just then we heard clear, but distant, shouts, "Hello there," repeated several times. The voices came from the top of that hill. In a clearing, we saw lights & what looked like a roof with smoke rising from a chimney.

As we finally located the voices, we recognized a very welcome invitation, "Comon up here!" We did. Lugging all our wet gear up the side of that muddy, slippery hill looked like a circus balancing act. We were exhausted.

After dumping all of those boxes & stuff on the porch, we were thrilled to be literally pulled into a cozy warm kitchen, wrapped in warm blankets & towels, & handed cups of hot chocolate. After a few minutes spent with introductions, & drying wet hair on those delicious warm towels, we were all ten of us seated at a big oak table filled with food. I asked why they had so much yummy food prepared for just the two of them.

Our laughing, grey haired host, puffed on his pipe, leaned back in his big red armchair, nodded to his sweet wife, & explained, "We were planning a big out-door family picnic, but our son's car wouldn't start, & then it started to rain, so, he called us to say, "Hey, Dad, we've called all the others, & they all agree it's best for all 38 of us to eat outside. So, we'll see ya' next Saturday. OK? Love ya'!" Everyone was happy but

my dear Delores. When we looked out & saw you folks in the rain....
Well, you saved the day! The food won't be wasted!"

His robust laugh, as he got up to hug his wife, warmed our hearts
even more than the warm blankets.

After the amazing, delicious meal, that dear man declared that he
would drive the two men to get our cars. He said he'd 'baby-sit' the
three canoes till they could be returned the next day. How thoughtful.
He refused any money for all the food, laundry & gasoline they
provided for us strangers.

We tried to clean up the mess, but Delores refused to let us wash the
stack of dishes. She put our jackets in the dryer & filled cartons with
food for us to take home. Those two people exuded love.

When the men returned, it was no surprise that everyone hugged
everyone, & tears were flowing. Our host asked us to join hands. He
prayed, praising God for new friends, & asking Jesus to guide us safely
home. It was a joyful ending to that eventful terribly wonderfully
terrible wonderful day. See why I'll never ever forget our canoe trip on
the Rifle River?

Nothing that happened that day could be called a miracle, but it
surely was a pile of sweet blessings.

DEFINE HAPPINESS

I've found a lot of thoughts in different places that help to define
something that many think is truly indefinable. Let's consider those
dozens of ideas & opinions.

Real happiness is made up of little things:

A smile...a hug...a moment of shared laughter...a sincere "I love
you"...a photo of loved ones, a raise in pay...the gift of truth &
faith...sometimes the sheer joy of being alive...a real letter in my
hands...the warm love-light in the eyes of someone special...that
special scent of fresh rain...the first smile of a new baby...to awaken
rested after a good night's sleep...the sound of laughter of kid's at
play...the closet is finally cleaned...the fantastic view of those stars...
the realization that the God who placed them there, also keeps them
there...and He loves me...sweet silence when we need it... A tiny dew
drop that reflects sunshine & the blue sky...the ability to help others in
need...the joy of learning new things in the old; and old things in the
new...the special joy that comes when we forgive someone, or when
someone forgives us...the great realization that God never lies, never

breaks His promises. He will satisfy us, meet all our needs, & always keep His word....If we remain flexible, we don't get bent out of shape ...

This endless list could fill a dozen books of a thousand pages each.

Let's shift gears, & try to remember what the Bible says too, about happiness.

Philippians 2 tells us that agreeing & working together with sympathetic hearts is great, & we need to be caring unselfish, & interested in others. That all sounds like a recipe for happiness to me. Then, if we pull some ideas from Phil. 4: 4 thru 19. It sounds even better. "Rejoice in the Lord always: and again I say, Rejoice."

Fix your thoughts on what is true & honorable & right. Think about things that are excellent & worthy of praise....And this same God who takes care of me will supply all your needs from His glorious riches in Christ Jesus."

I read somewhere that God's faithfulness isn't only, & all, in the skies. It starts with us & reaches the skies. Bob's mom told us, "The desire for more or better possessions is really a longing to fill an empty place in life. So, to have true happiness, true joy...

We can be happy with what we have today, if we realize that it's just what we're s'posed to have today. It is enough. God is enough; and all we need tomorrow shouldn't come to us today."

Happiness is not getting what we want; it's recognizing what we already have.

Happiness is not saying, "I don't have time for"...but rather it is realizing that time is sooo precious it's only given to us "moment by moment".

If the soul constantly seeks happiness, where is the peace & joy? When we rest in Him, those circumstances, & things that surround us, are of little account. When we finally grasp His hand, He will never want to let go. And, we shouldn't.

To know that God understands our prayers even when we can't find words to tell Him...WOW! Best of all, He leans down to us & LISTENS.

It's been said "God's peace is joy resting. His joy is peace dancing" That sounds even better than what we commonly call happiness.

We can't be truly happy if we wait to see how things turn out; but only if we're certain that, in God's care, wisdom & love, the tangled things will make sense regardless of how they turn out. If it's HIS way, it's the BEST way. We usually don't understand that in advance, only as we look back on it.

I've heard folks snicker & sneer at those of us who reminisce. I don't mind being called an "old fogey." If we are sure & secure in knowing who we are...and ...WHOSE we are, people can call us anything...& we quickly recognize that it is their problem, not ours.

Let's share more opinions of REAL HAPPINESS, more of my collection...no idea who said these things...but I still enjoy them.

We often refer to self-confidence, but, perhaps we'd be happier if we realize we need God-confidence. He has lavished so much on us...we dare not give ourselves credit for what He has done...& continues to do...for us, in us, & through us.

Because God created us in His own image, then, being creative (using the gifts & creativity He gave us) should certainly make us happy.

If I'm not happy, & if my heart is broken, God can fix it, if I give Him all the pieces.

Birds don't sing because they are happy. They sing because they have a song. If that is their job...then, what is my job?

A good definition of happiness: Happiness depends on happenings & our reaction to them. Joy, which is truer, deeper, richer, more satisfying & longer lasting...depends on Christ & our relationship to Him.

Now that I know all that, I should be better able to recognize & define happiness & joy. I now aim for, yearn for, & hope for both! Those who bring joy to others, even in the smallest ways, can't keep it from splashing on themselves.

Could we agree that the opposite of joy often resembles grumbling? Some folks grumble without suffering; others suffer without grumbling. I believe that the JOY OF JESUS makes the difference.

I've heard that he who growls all day is bound to be dog-tired at night.

Proverbs 17:22 states, "A merry heart doeth good like a medicine: but a broken spirit drieth the bones."

In I John 1:4 when Jesus is discussing the Christian believer's life, he says, "And these things write we unto you, that your joy may be full."

People are hungry for good cheer in these difficult economic times.

"Our feeling is that humor is a powerful evangelistic tool, a peacemaking tool." It's been said. "We've gotten so heavily theologized and psychologized that we can't see the humor anymore. We're blind to it."

Paul talks about singing, "Rejoice in the Lord; again I say, rejoice."

Another scripture verse says "The joy of the Lord is my strength" YES!

A man is a success if he gets up in the morning and goes to bed at night and in between does what he wants to do.
Bob Dylan

THIS IS FOUR ALL

We'll begin with a box, and the plural is boxes; but the plural of ox became oxen not oxes. One fowl is a goose, but two are called geese, yet the plural of moose should never be meese. You may find a lone mouse or a nest full of mice; yet the plural of house is houses, not hice.

If the plural of man is always called men, why shouldn't the plural of pan be called pen? If I spoke of my foot and show you my feet, and I give you a boot, would a pair be called beet? If one is a tooth and a whole set are teeth, why shouldn't the plural of booth be called beeth?

Then one may be that, and three would be those, yet hat in the plural would never be hose, and the plural of cat is cats, not cose. We speak, of a brother and also or brethren, but though we say mother, we never say methren.

Then the masculine pronouns are he, his and him, but imagine the feminine, she, shis and shim.

Let's face it, English is a crazy language.

There is no egg in eggplant nor ham in hamburger; neither apple nor pine in pineapple. English muffins weren't invented in England.

————————

We take English for granted.

————————

But if we explore its paradoxes, we find that quicksand can work slowly, boxing rings are square and a guinea pig is neither from Guinea nor is it a pig.

————————

And why is it that writers write, but fingers don't fing, grocers don't groce, and hammers don't ham?

————————

Doesn't it seem crazy that you can make amends, but not one amend?

————————

If you have a bunch of odds and ends and get rid of all but one of them, what do you call it?

————————

If teachers taught, why didn't preachers praught?
Why do we park in the driveway & drive in the parkway? Why are black & white newspapers read all over?

————————

If you're seeking excellent advice ask an expert.
If you seek wisdom ask a scholar.
If you seek honesty ask a kid.

FOR THOSE "SPARE" MOMENTS

Ponder this:

- If lawyers are disbarred and clergymen defrocked, doesn't it follow that electricians can be delighted, musicians denoted, cowboys deranged, models deposed, tree surgeons debarked, and dry cleaners depressed?
- Ever wonder about those people who spend $2.00 a piece on those little bottles of Evian water? Try spelling Evian backwards: Naïve.
- If 4 out of 5 people SUFFER from diarrhea, does that mean that one enjoys it?
- When we say HE, HIS and HIM...why not say SHE, SHIS & SHIM?
- If people from Poland are called Poles, why aren't people from Holland called Holes
- Why do we say something is out of whack? What's a whack?
- Do infants enjoy infancy as much as adults enjoy adultery?
- If a pig loses its voice, is it disgruntled?
- If love is blind, why is lingerie so popular?
- Why is the man who invests all your money called a broker?
- Why do croutons come in airtight packages? Aren't they just stale bread to begin with?
- When cheese gets its picture taken, what does it say?
- Why are a wise man and a wise guy opposite things?
- Why do overlook and oversee mean opposite things?
- Why isn't the number 11 pronounced onety one?
- Do Lipton Tea employees take coffee breaks?
- What hair color do they put on the driver's licenses of bald men?
- Whatever happened to Preparations A through G?

THE TEN COMMANDMENTS OF HOW TO GET ALONG WITH PEOPLE

1. Keep skid chains on your tongue. Always say less than you think. Cultivate a low, persuasive voice. How you say it often counts more than what you say.
2. Make promises sparingly, and keep them faithfully, no matter what the cost.
3. Never let an opportunity pass to say a kind and encouraging word to or about somebody. Praise good work, regardless of who did it. If criticism is needed, offer it gently, never harshly.

4. Be interested in others, their pursuits, their work, their homes and families. Make merry with those who rejoice, and weep with those who mourn. Let everyone you meet, however humble, feel that you regard him or her as a person of importance.
5. Be cheerful. Don't burden or depress those around you by dwelling on your minor aches and pains and small disappointments. Remember, everyone is carrying some kind of burden, often heavier than your own.
6. Keep an open mind. Discuss, but don't argue. It is a mark of superior mind to be able to disagree without being disagreeable.
7. Let your virtues, if you have any, speak for themselves. Refuse to talk of another's vices. Discourage gossip. It is a waste of valuable time.
8. Be careful of another's feelings. Wit and humor at another person's expense may do more damage than you will ever know.
9. Pay no attention to disparaging remarks. Remember, the person who carried the message may not be the most accurate reporter in the world, and things become twisted in the retelling. Live so that nobody will believe them.
10. Nervous tension and bad digestion are common causes of backbiting.
11. Don't be too eager to get the credit due you. Do your best, and be patient. Forget about yourself, and let others "remember." Success is much sweeter that way.
   Ann Landers

MATURITY

* Maturity is the ability to control anger and settle differences without violence.
* Maturity is patience. It is the willingness to pass up immediate pleasure in favor of a long-term gain.
* Maturity is perseverance, the ability to sweat out a project or a situation in spite of heavy opposition and discouraging setbacks.
* Maturity is the capacity to face unpleasantness and frustration, discomfort and defeat, without complaint or collapse.
* Maturity is being big enough to say, "I was wrong." And, when right, the mature person need not experience the satisfaction of saying, "I told you so."
* Maturity is the ability to make a decision and stand by it. The im-

mature spend their lives exploring endless possibilities and then do nothing.

- Maturity means dependability, keeping one's word and coming through in a crisis. The immature are masters of the alibi. They are the confused and the conflicted. Their lives are a maze of broken promises, former friends, unfinished business and good intentions that somehow never materialize.
- Maturity is the art of living in peace with what we cannot change, the courage to change what should be changed and the wisdom to know the difference. **Ann Landers**

Some people praise others in order to elevate the others; while some praise others in order to put themselves on a level with them; the first is a form of homage, and the second a form of snobbery.

The generality of men sometimes seems divided into those who can't remember a joke, and those who can't remember anything else.

It is the superstition of the modern "educated" person to believe that science can "explain" what faith cannot; but if the so-called explanations of science are pursued far enough, they are seen to be as tendentious and, in their own way, as mystical, as the more traditional explanations, and...even harder to believe.

Sermons make us feel good when they make us feel bad; having felt bad, we then feel free to go out again and commit those deeds that will call for more sermons to repeat the process ad infinitum.

We are all proud of the vices we don't have; it is certain that Jack the Ripper prided himself upon the fact that he has never stooped so low as to attack a child. **Sydney J. Harris**

Abraham Lincoln Said. . .

- You cannot bring about prosperity by discouraging thrift.
- You cannot strengthen the weak by weakening the strong.
- You cannot help the wage earner by pulling down the wage payer.
- You cannot further brotherhood by encouraging class hatred.
- You cannot establish sound security by spending more than you earn.

• You cannot build character and courage by taking away man's initiative and independence.

How I wish today's leaders understood the wisdom of Abe's words!

Kindness is the only service that will stand the storm of life and not wash out. It will wear well, look well and be remembered long after the prism of politeness or the complexion of courtesy has faded away.
When I am gone, I hope it can be said of me that I plucked a thistle and planted a flower wherever I thought a flower would grow.
A. Lincoln

Character is like a tree and reputation like its shadow. The shadow is what we think of it; the tree is the real thing.
A. Lincoln

The greatest pictures and statues have been painted and chiseled in words.
Robert Ingersoll

A powerful agent is the right word.
Mark Twain

The hottest places in hell are reserved for those who, in a time of great moral crisis, maintain their neutrality.
Dante

Suffering is everywhere. So is the lasting & thrilling joy of helping to overcome it.

When my great-grandfather became a centenarian, a newspaper reporter asked him how he felt. "Fine," Grandpa replied. "In fact, I get around better now than I did a hundred years ago."

————————

I would rather have one little rose from the garden of a friend than to have the choicest flowers when my stay on earth must end. I would rather have one pleasant word in kindness said to me, than flattery when my heart is still and life has ceased to be. Bring me all your flowers today whether pink or white or red. I'd rather have one blossom now than a truckload when I'm dead.

—————————

"No man is an island." What would we do without a friend with whom to laugh, cry, share, and dream? A British publication once offered a prize for the best definition of a friend. The winning response was: "A friend is the one who comes in when the whole world has gone out." So what makes a friend so valuable? True friendship demonstrates availability, dependability, vulnerability, and responsibility. We must be willing to be there in both the good times and bad; when our friends are struggling and when we go through a hardship and need help. Our genuine friends will love us despite our problems.

Friends aren't perfect, however, and sometimes they fail us. Proverbs 18:24 says, "A man that hath friends must shew himself friendly: and there is a friend that sticketh closer than a brother." Jesus is the best friend we could ever have. His love is unconditional and His availability is endless.

—————————

Life doesn't begin at 40, or at 20, but at Calvary.
Not only does Jesus add years to your life,
He adds life to your years.

—————————

Satan drags us down to his level. God lifts us up to His.

—————————

I know you believe you understand what you think I said but I am not sure you realize that what you heard is not what I meant.

MY CONFESSION
I only hope we find God again before it is too late!!
By: Ben Stein

"I am a Jew, and every single one of my ancestors was Jewish. And it does not bother me even a little bit when people call those beautiful, lit up, bejeweled trees, Christmas trees. I don't feel threatened. I don't feel discriminated against. That's what they are, Christmas trees.

It doesn't bother me a bit when people say, "Merry Christmas" to me. I don't think they are slighting me or getting ready to put me in a ghetto. In fact, I kind of like it. It shows that we are all brothers and sisters celebrating this happy time of year. It doesn't bother me at all that there is a manger scene on display at a key intersection near my beach house in Malibu. If people want a crèche, it's just as fine with me as it is the Menorah a few hundred yards away.

I don't like getting pushed around for being a Jew, and I don't think Christians like getting pushed around for being Christians. I think people who believe in God are sick and tired of getting pushed around, period. I have no idea where the concept came from, that America is an explicitly atheist country. I can't find it in the Constitution and I don't like it being shoved down my throat.

Or maybe I can put it another way: where did the idea come from that we should worship celebrities and we aren't allowed to worship God as we understand Him? I guess that's a sign that I'm getting old, too. But there are a lot of us who are wondering where these celebrities came from and where the America we knew went to."

Billy Graham's daughter was interviewed on the Early Show and Jane Clayson asked her, "How could God let something like this happen?" (regarding Hurricane Katrina). Anne Graham gave an extremely profound and insightful response. She said, "I believe God is deeply saddened by this, just as we are, but for years we've been telling God to get out of our schools, to get out of our government and to get out of our lives. And being the gentleman He is, I believe He has calmly backed out. How can we expect God to give us His blessing and His protection if we demand He leave us alone?"

In light of recent events...terrorists attack, school shootings, etc. I think it started when Madeleine Murray O'Hare (she was murdered, her body found a few years ago) complained she didn't want prayer in our schools, and we said OK. Then someone said you better not read the Bible in school. And we said OK. The Bible says thou shalt not kill; thou shalt not steal, and love your neighbor as yourself.

Then Dr. Benjamin Spock said we shouldn't spank our children when they misbehave, because their little personalities would be warped and we might damage their self-esteem (Dr. Spock's son committed suicide). We said an expert should know what he's talking about. And we said OK.

Now, we're asking ourselves why our children have no conscience, why they don't know right from wrong, and why it doesn't bother them to kill strangers, their classmates, and themselves.

Probably, if we think about it long and hard enough, we can figure it out. I think it has a great deal to do with, "WE REAP WHAT WE SOW."

Funny how simple it is for people to trash God and then wonder why the world's going to hell. Funny how we believe what the newspapers say, but question what the Bible says. Funny how you can send 'jokes' through email and they spread like wildfire, but when you start sending messages regarding the Lord, people think twice about sharing. Funny how lewd, crude, vulgar and obscene articles pass freely through cyberspace, but public discussion of God is suppressed in the school and workplace.

THE KITCHEN

"Mom, C'mon into my private office so we can talk, OK?" The eager look on that 18 year old face prompted his Mom to give him her full attention. He sat on the edge of the large round table in the center of the big old ugly pink kitchen. He didn't even notice the hot pink walls that clashed with the dark, rusty orange colored stained wooden cupboards. But, even in her earnest desire to hear whatever he had to share, it was hard to ignore that awful color scheme. She stood, facing him, backed up against the too-low, too-small, too-stained sink, with the noisy faucets, & listened intently to his thoughts & plans.

Rented houses aren't all that bad, and, kids never seem to mind as much as moms do anyway. In fact, family & friends seemed to gravitate to that ugly old pink room. We often wondered who chose the vivid color that was the worst possible choice for the wooden cupboards. The floor was about six shades of bright red & blue & green & yellow & purple & orange, and no, pink. YUCK! – But it was a rented house.

However, the chores of cooking & cleaning became lost in the warmth & joys of happy times. Bread-baking smells; laughter of large groups of teens, eating homemade soup & sandwiches after their song fests around the old piano; & oodles of kids making big messes during

134

the "cookie factories," the day after Thanksgiving, every year.

Perhaps the sweetest memories came as Mom & Gramma shared coffee time at the big table, many mornings. Mom was a very new Christian, & she truly enjoyed the precious truths & blessings they shared, while learning to pray & laugh & cry...and...praise Jesus...together.

The too small window, with white eyelet curtains, looked over & past the troubled lives of the neighbors, to a row of huge majestic blue spruce trees. Their serene, strong beauty helped to transform a sink full of greasy pots & pans, into a vehicle of travel, to truly transport Mom from those hum-drum duties. Her chariot of joy left the pink kitchen behind, & enhanced the possibility that precious conversations & charming anecdotes could even be written down for the kids to read, & re-read, to remember & tell to their own kids & grandkids.

Mom can still see those crooked, wobbly old chairs with chipped paint, & the horrid color scheme. BUT, Gram's Christ – centered words & loving attitude which taught the three kids, (plus their dozens of friends and parents alike) that ugly pink walls can even help us to laughingly imagine God's lovely pink sunsets.

Once, when the teenage son stopped by Gram's bedroom, after his date, he invited her down to the kitchen for cookies & conversation that lasted till 4 a.m.!

It became obvious that the ugly pink kitchen had a charm all its own. That big table & crooked chairs would sure have some stories to tell, if only they could talk. Perhaps the people who sat there might be considered actors on the stage of life.

But, because of Gram's words and actions, Jesus was glorified & love spilled out of that ugly pink kitchen.

IT'S ADDICTIVE

One of the big houses we lived in during Bob's army years in Texas was divided in half. We shared a big bathroom, & the other half of the house, with an army dentist & his clever wife from Massachusetts.

We became good friends, sharing meals, movies, trips to museums & picnics for several months. After we learned that they called themselves Christian Scientists, we didn't discuss religion very often. Once they praised Mary Baker Eddy & her inspirational writings, told us they did not believe in illness, & warned us (lovingly) not to tell them about Jesus, as that was all fake ideas, for uneducated people. So, we didn't.

But we prayed for them.

One day Janet fell, broke one leg & one ankle. When we visited her in the army hospital it was truly awkward. What do you say to someone who has both legs in traction, high over the bed, claiming she is fine & will be home soon?

We took Janet flowers & prepared meals for Duncan. A week later Bob was transferred & we moved away. But we did keep in touch over the years from Michigan to Massachusetts & back, via Christmas cards & little notes.

After about ten years we got a January 'fone call from Janet. She said, "Ya know, Duncan & I always did resent the way you wrote Bible verses on your Christmas cards.* That is, till this last time. I yelled at him & said I was sick of it. He told me not to yell at him, but to look up what those dumb verses said. I guess it made me madder that you wrote the reference but didn't say what it really said in the Bible. Sooo I ran next door & borrowed a Bible to look it up." She paused, "Just finding the dumb verses was hard work for us. But, I've gotta' tell you, we were shocked when we read what they said. Duncan & I thought the Bible was full of "Thou shall nots" & we couldn't believe that it said you thanked God for our friendship & prayed for us. WOW! We were so s'prised that we decided to read more of it. I guess you know it is addictive, doncha?" She only stopped talking long enough to take a breath & for me to agree with her.

Then she added, "Well, any way, our neighbor, that we borrowed the Bible from, brought us a new one as a gift & told us to start reading John, Acts, & Philippians first. We truly are excited, & just want you & Bob to know...and...thanks for patiently praying for us. Gotta' go to work. Love ya' bye!"

I sat crying & praising God. That was probly' in 1955 or '56. They drove here to visit us in 1985...and visited again in 2001.

They moved Duncan's dental clinic to a big lodge on a mountain in Vermont, so his patients could have picnics in their huge backyard. Janet & Duncan accepted Christ & became active members in their church till they died. I wonder if she still plays the organ in Heaven. They don't need a dentist up there, but he was an expert with woodworking tools & maybe is carving things of wood from the forest & trees he loved.

- Philippians 1:2-4 "Grace be unto you, and peace, from God our Father, and from the Lord Jesus Christ. I thank my God upon every remembrance of you, Always in every prayer of mine for you all making request with joy,"

- Ephesians 1:2 "Grace be to you, and peace, from God our Father, and from the Lord Jesus Christ."

- Colossians 1:3 "We give thanks to God and the Father of our Lord Jesus Christ, praying always for you,"

GROWING HOBBIES

It's fascinating to learn of the collections, interests, and hobbies all around us. There seems to be no end to the variety nor to the way we all get involved. My story is not unusual, but the results of my hobby became exciting.

A friend from grade school recently told me she remembers seeing me cut out letters from scrap paper when we were in 4th grade together. That was a shock to me, but it was no surprise to her, to learn that I have now turned that silly childhood pastime into an adult hobby, as well as a profitable avocation.

Back at Cooley High School in Detroit in 1938 there was a very special art teacher. Dorthea Probst always searched for a particular gift, or a spark of interest, in each of her pupils, & fanned it into a flame. Not many youngsters found it fun to cut out letters from scrap paper. She kept me after school for at least an hour every day, claiming she needed my help. We both knew who was giving & who was getting help. I wish I had told her that her efforts weren't wasted...wish I could tell her now that her tireless use of time to help me, & that her love of color & artistic design rubbed off on me to become part of the creativity, skills & perseverance I've needed since.

Another teacher in high school, who tried to hone my skills in sewing, had no idea what the results would be. I wish I could apologize to her for being less than the obedient sewing pupil she hoped us all to be. But, my sister & I sewed at home on Gramma's old treadle sewing machine, & I was never patient enough to do things the teacher's way...by the rules?...Never!

But, sewing became a useful tool, & the proverbial "means to an end," that I unknowingly sought. Because money was so scarce at home, I went behind her back, & that teacher truly resented it. She didn't understand.

My hard-working Daddy brought home only $10.00 for two weeks and over-time. A prom dress was not possible, so, at age 15, I entered a city-wide contest for all high school students, with consent of their sewing teachers. Three major department stores supplied patterns, fabrics, publicity & judges. Simple items to wear to school were required for entry. My sewing teacher was shocked & angry to learn that I was making a Prom Dress. Judges for the style show came from the three major newspapers also.

At the last moment, while we were on the runway, all of the judges changed the scheduled three prizes & awarded me a fourth prize, even though I broke the rules & made a Prom Dress. After all, they agreed, it was for a school prom. I still have that pale green dotted swiss dress, with miles & miles of skirt (I doubled what the pattern called for), but I long ago forgot what the prize was. I wonder if that sewing teacher ever forgave me.

That same year, the art teacher urged me to make a tiny living room in a shoe-box, to enter in a county wide competition of miniatures, at the Detroit Institute of Art. What a thrill for me, as a young teen, to be a part of that wondrous exhibit...and... my entry won honorable mention! The sweet smell of success is addictive, I'm told.

Art classes & sewing projects were put on hold for awhile. Bob & I spent over three years in Texas. As an army wife, moving constantly from town to town, I had no sewing machine, nor anything to sew on...till a new idea arose.

Bob was Assistant Commanding Officer at a camp near Austin, Texas, for German Prisoners of War. A nearby rancher was so grateful for help he received in his rice fields, from the POW's, that he offered me all of the feed sacks I could carry. They were brightly colored, stripes, checks & flowers galore.

The prisoners heard of my plight & spent hours & hours to clean & repair a very old, very large sewing machine used for making shoes! They searched every where till they found a needle for it, & then presented it to me with a grand gesture, suited for a queen. Of course, their ulterior motive became obvious when they brought some of those colorful feed sacks, & showed me photos of a wife or girl friend or Mother, back in Germany. I spoke no German, they spoke very little English, but we did communicate. Aprons, blouses, & pillowcases by the dozen, came off that silly old sewing machine, as those German fellas grinned gladly. That sewing teacher would have been pleased.

After we returned to Michigan, my sewing skills were forced to grow with drapes & bed spreads & three fast growing kids to dress, and very little money.

I assumed that everyone could sew, except my Mother, so it was a surprise when I was offered jobs in three large, up-scale department stores, plus the YWCA, the YMCA, an elegant fur salon, & JoAnn's Fabric Store. I soon learned that those of us who choose to sew (& like it), are so rare that we're becoming extinct. We are in demand in the job market.

A while later, I started an alteration business in my basement. The money rolled in, & I had more customers than I could handle. My rules were "two days a week between nine and six," and, I never strayed from that. One good customer called me an hour late. I asked if he ever called the drugstore or J.C. Penney's after they closed. He understood & showed up at nine the next morning, smiling broadly.

Meanwhile, some ladies from my church, & I, made large banners for the churches, for Red Cross, for Habitat for Humanity, & for Delta College. That was delightful spare time fun. We decorated bulletin boards in many places & loved it.

But everything changed when offers came to teach on a college campus, even though I've never gone to college. The first courses were "Sew for Profit", "Cash in on Your Sewing Skills", "Start an Alteration Business", "Tailoring", and "Linings or Relinings." It was great fun to get paid for doing what I loved to do.

Then, one day, on campus, I was shocked to have an invitation to teach my true favorites. The new classes were the ones Mrs. Probst had unknowingly prepared me for, in 1938 & '39. The titles were "Creative Banners and Wall Hangings", "How to Make Your Bulletin Board Say What You Want it to Say", & "The Creativity of Chrismons." Hurrah!

The skills of using colors to speak a message, making letters of hundred of sizes & styles, creating stories with creativity, to be seen, not just spoken...plus the facts of balance & design...ignite the excitement that cannot be put into words.

I'm constantly amazed that teens & adults from various places, have hired me to teach "Creative Banners" classes for many purposes & styles. It's gratifying to receive photos of the results of their creativity. Months & years later I'm still in awe of their God-given talents that I tried to hone, as my teachers did. The originality, skills, enthusiasm, as well as significant efforts, produce meaningful results that still thrill me. Sometimes to tears of joy.

One banner that our team submitted in a nationwide competition won first prize, which was a thousand dollar, week long trip.

Some banners are made of satin, lame', velvet, taffeta, burlap, sequins, & fringes of all styles & colors. Many took 60 to 80 hours, for a team of four or more, to complete. They hang now in schools, churches, Red Cross buildings, colleges, homes, etc. Some hang in Florida, Washington, Wisconsin, Poland, Mexico, the Philippines, & who knows where else? And they started in the creative minds & hearts of kids, teens & adults in mid-Michigan.

Or...did they really start in that art teacher's heart in Detroit, who nurtured the joy & creativity in all her students? My hobby has become profitable, useful, beautiful, fun, fulfilling, long lasting...and...proof that teachers can bring out the best in their students, for centuries to come.

So, find your own gifts & fan that wee spark, to light more corners than you can imagine. I failed at typing & singing, & many other things...But...not everything. Thank the Lord!

SEW SPECIAL

On Mondays and Thursdays from 9 a.m. to 6 p.m., a lot of people came to my basement workroom for the alterations I could do on their clothing. My business was called SEW SPECIAL.

One morning a lady I didn't know, dragged a huge black plastic bag in & thumped it down the steps. After three more trips to her car, she said, "I'm Ruth, I work in the busy office of a doctor, & have no time to do my mending. Every item has a safety pin to show what needs to be done. I used a zillion pins." She plopped herself down into a chair breathlessly.

I pulled out a few things from the first bag, & commented, "I charge one dollar minimum for each item. If this shirt only needs a button, I'd be happy to give you some buttons ...."

Ruth interrupted me with an enthusiastic, "I do not own a needle & do not plan to buy one! Please just fix 'em all...OK?"

About three o'clock I called her to say, "I just want you to know that I've already done $47.00 worth. Are you sure you don't want to borrow a needle? I'd be happy to teach you how to sew on a button."

She laughed & flippantly answered, "I'll gladly pay whatever it costs, just do 'em, OK? Call me when they're done." She slammed down the 'fone. Pants to be shortened & a coat to be relined etc., brought the totals up on Ruth's four big bags. It was $86.00 the first day, $103 the second day, & $98 the third day. Ruth became a good customer, who brought smaller batches after that.

The man who owned the corner gas station said he had "discovered gold", when I shortened his pants, & all his uniforms. When he sent me many of his customers, I became very busy.

It was great to be able to do all the sewing at home while baking casseroles, (& even homemade bread at times) making soup and...to be there when our kids got home from school. We always kept things in a business like manner, except for the kitchen aromas, cuz, after all, it was a business. A good arrangement.

My husband Bob urged, "Don't over do it, you don't really need to earn more than the Mayor does." I assured him there was no danger of that, but I was glad he approved. Sewing was always my favorite sport.

Often the customers were strangers. One gentleman tried on his trousers, waited (not very patiently) as I marked the length on one leg, & then burst away to remove the pants. I quickly asked, "Sir, do you want me to shorten both legs?" "Of course!" he barked. "Then you'd best let me mark both legs!" I answered.

He was soooo annoyed. No one had ever told him that before. A week later when he picked them up, he was still annoyed. But, the next week he came back with three pairs of pants, and, with a sly grin said, "Perhaps you'll adjust these for me. The last fella' who did my pants only marked one leg, they were never even." He gave me a generous tip & a big grin.

Another customer I had not met before, came to have her very expensive coat shortened. Her name was Margaret. As I marked the length, she gasped, "Oh dear!" and grabbed the table.

I helped her to the chair, brought her a drink of water, & asked, "Are you OK? Shall I call someone to come & get you?"

"No," she murmured, with her head down in her hands. She refused any other help.

"Is it OK if I pray for you?" I asked. She shrugged, silently.

How should I pray for someone I don't know, & what was wrong? So, I just started –

"Dear Father, please intercede for my new friend. Help her to feel better, & I ask dear Lord, that You will meet every one of her needs. If she needs some sort of doctor or medicine, make that clear to her. And, Thank You Lord for all that You're going to do, in the strong , loving name of Jesus, Amen."

As she stood to leave, I reached to hug her. It was like hugging a tree; firm, hard, cold. I walked her to her car. She slammed the door & drove off. I prayed, "Father, bless her in every way. Does she need to make Jesus her best friend?"

Many weeks passed & Margaret did not come to get her coat. About four months later, a lady came down stairs, & I didn't recognize her, so I asked where she had gotten my name, I was shocked to learn that I was talking to Margaret!

Her curt comment was, "I was sure it was a mistake to let you pray for me that first day!" My head was swimming & I was speechless.

Then, calmly Margaret sat down & finished the story; a smile came. "The day I was here, I felt so bad that I drove directly to the emergency room. After a brief exam, they admitted me. I was truly mad at you! Then after a million tests, they learned my doctor was giving me the wrong medicine! I was sharing a room with a lady who talked too much. She drove me batty. Then she prayed for me too. We became friends. She lives two blocks from me. I now attend her church. Last week I asked Jesus to be my Savior & my friend. So, Betty, God really did meet all my needs...Say, the coat looks great." & she gave me a big warm hug.

BARGAINS

Salesladies at the fabric store knew how often I searched for bargains of bright colored fabrics & items for the banners classes I taught at several places, all year long. So, it came as no surprise when I heard, "Hey, Betty, look at the variety of colors in this big sale. We hoped you'd come in before we sold out. Look...every color of the rainbow & a few besides!"

So, of course, I filled the cart with a bolt of each, ignoring the black one. We'd never make a black banner. But...can't pass up such a terrific bargain. Maybe a coat lining with that black piece?

Entering the work room, the sack was so full & so heavy, it was hard to handle. A fellow banner maker, frowning, asked, "What's the black piece for? Does that go home with you?"

"Maybe a coat lining," I muttered.

Another team member, helping to unpack & fold the new treasures, joked, "WOW, never saw a black banner, but innovations are worth considering."

They both grinned & put the black fabric back in the bag for me to take home, later.

During the next few months we used the lovely fall colors for a Thanksgiving banner, plus two Christmas ones, & used the traditional colors. One was red & white with metallic gold trims. The other was a dark blue night scene with a crude cradle, & a huge silver star among tiny stars. Then we all rested a while.

In January, the Pastor asked about our plans for the Lenten season. We had none. His focus & theme would be THE CROSS. He offered a few familiar Bible verses & left the room, smiling, and saying, "I'm depending on your creativity. The Lord will show y'all what He wants." Several times previously our Pastor had shown us a photo & asked if we could make a banner of it. Our answer often was, "No...but God can...& I'm sure He will show us how"...and...He always did. BUT, this time all four of us drew a blank, as we sat staring out the window. Nothing. Blank paper, blank stares. Let's meet next Thursday, usual time. The usual thrill & excitement seemed to be missing.

On Thursday we still had no ideas. We prayed again. Nothing. Sorting through that stack of rich lovely colors of satin & taffeta fabrics...we kept seeking ideas. Nothing. No ideas. We all felt empty.

The bag I had forgotten to take home, those many weeks before, fell off the shelf & the black fabric slid out in a lovely shimmering dark pile on the floor. As though rehearsed, two of the ladies softly shouted, "That's it!!"

"What's it?" we others asked, in unison.

They both remembered seeing a foto in an ad from a Christian bookstore with a black banner; but where was it? They found the magazine & turned page after page. Sure 'nuff they found it; we got an idea from it & started applying that idea to our own situation. We knew it was right.

None of our previous ideas were even close to working here. Bit by bit it started to form. We placed three layers of black net to form a cross, five feet tall by three feet wide, on the black fabric background we'd made six feet tall by four feet wide. Next, strange as it seemed, we outlined that big black net cross with black sequins. How odd it looked to all of us, but we knew it was right. No doubt. None of us knew why, but it was right.

Then we placed a crown of thorns at the very top...made of two shades of beige & tan burlap (in third dimension for depth).

Large silver letters at the bottom said, "ONCE FOR ALL." Good, but...something was missing. As we all stood puzzled, a young teenager, rushing down the hall toward the gym, burst in, tipped her head to one side & declared, "It needs drops of blood!" And she left!!!

First, we used small red satin drops, but they looked like M & M candies, NO! We then found some dark red velvet, & cut three different sizes...with a point on top & wide across the rounded bottom. The 10 inch & 9 inch & 8 inch drops were just right. YES!

BUT, the entire banner hung crooked, & we couldn't straighten it. How do you straighten a six foot banner & make it stay straight? As the custodian walked down the hall, we asked for his suggestion. Before we even finished our request, he simply answered, "Large spikes!"

He grinned & left...we wondered how can we do that? Was he serious, or was he joking?

One team member rushed to a nearby hardware, & bought us five spikes - (that's all they had) at six inches long. Hung by invisible fishline across the bottom, they solved the problem, but also reminded us of the nails in Christ's hands & feet.

God knew why I bought that lovely piece of black fabric. Was it a bargain or a mystery or a miracle?

That amazing banner has blessed many people for years & years, but most of all, it blessed us! We had not really made it...He did it.

CREATIVITY (BY: The Christophers)
Makes thing happen

Where will my creativity be of use? Most of us have only to look around where we are, at inequities, at pain, at waste, at confusion – and ask if this has to be.

When we allow ourselves to be puzzled, to ask 'why?" we can start to make things happen rather than let them happen to us.

The refusal to take things for granted is the beginning of creative response. As we search for ways to bring order out of the disorder we see, we open the way for changing the world around us.

Parents ask why their community has a drug problem. They get the facts and the reasons for the susceptibility of neighborhood youngsters. With other parents, police and community resources, they look for positive alternatives.

A young person, disturbed by the ill humor of her grandmother, becomes aware of the elderly woman's empty life and helps her to find an absorbing hobby.

A teacher, dismayed by her students' apathy, reexamines her own attitude and her methods. She finds new ways to reach the young people and the class comes alive.

CREATIVITY
May be blocked

Attitudes and mental habits that stifle creativity have been cited by Executives' Digest:

1. Excessive need for order. This encourages inflexible thinking and discourages originality.
2. Reluctance to play – with things, ideas, words, people. Individuals who are afraid of "looking silly" rarely innovate.
3. Resource myopia. Society values realism, i.e., seeing things as they are, whereas innovation requires seeing things as they might be.
4. Reluctance to risk. Innovation depends on a willingness to stick one's neck out.
5. Reluctance to exert influence. Fear of seeming "pushy" results in acceptance of the established way of doing things, even when there is a better way.
6. Overcertainty. The "disease of specialists" – those who are experts or think they are – closes the mind to new approaches.

How open are you?

CREATIVITY
Is a way of life

In 1928, British bacteriologist, Sir Alexander Fleming was engaged in research on influenza. He noticed that mold had developed accidentally on a culture plate. It had created a bacteria-free circle around itself. This observation led to his Nobel prize-winning discovery of penicillin.

Important insights are rarely accidents. Creativity thrives in the presence of: **Awareness.** We are most deeply aware, say psychologists, in the areas in which we are most intensely committed.

Curiosity. Searching for the "how' and "why' of things broadens our perspective. It nurtures our ability to judge.

Openness to new ideas. Inventor Thomas Alva Edison once said: "I'll try anything. I'll even try Limburger cheese!" The more we can keep the door open for a flow of ideas, the better the chance for usable solutions.

Patience with being unsettled. In the process of letting go of old answers and comfortable patterns, there is anxiety. It is akin to the chemical process of fermentation which brings into being a new substance.

Sense of humor. Humor contains the same opposing elements found in most definitions of creative behavior: playfulness and seriousness, originality and reality, nonsense and purpose, the irrational and the rational.

Living creatively is being ready for almost anything!

CREATIVITY
Use it

"Can you tell me who made you?" the preacher asked the small boy. The youngster thought a moment. Then he looked up at the preacher and said, "God made part of me."

"What do you mean, 'part of you?'"

"Well," answered the boy, "God made me little. I grew the rest myself."

"Growing the rest" is a lifetime job for all of us.

God has fitted each of us to live one life, our own. We find personal wholeness and joy in discovering and using the particular gifts He has given us for living that life. And we make a difference.

"We are collaborators in creation," wrote Teilhard de Chardin. What you and I are becoming is what the world is becoming.

CREATIVITY

Painter Georgia O'Keeffe was the subject of a television special honoring her 90th birthday.

In this portrait of the artist, Ms. O'Keeffe said that she had tried in her youth to find someone to teach her how to paint landscapes.

Finally she stopped trying.

"They could tell me how they painted their landscapes," she said. "But they couldn't tell me how to paint mine."

Each person has something different to offer.

In painting a picture or living a life, to create an "original" is, in great part, to work with the nature God has provided you and to reveal your uniqueness.

CREATIVITY
You have it

Psychologists have found that only about two percent of adults use their creativity, compared with 10 percent of seven-year-old children. When five-year-olds were tested, the results soared to 90 percent!

Originality is a way of life for the small child. But something happens on the way to adulthood. Whatever that is, it is a fact that most of us settle down to living with worn concepts and set thinking patterns. The daring and the delight are gone. So is the originality. They needn't be.

Experts claim that it is never too late to tap our creativity.

Professor Sidney Parnes, professor of creative studies at New York's State University College at Buffalo, says, "All of us can learn to better understand and appreciate our own creative potential, as well as to nurture it more fully in individuals and groups for whom we have responsibility."

According to Professor Parnes, it doesn't take genius. It means taking what we see and know and putting it together in a new way that makes sense and that works.

CREATIVITY
Looks for new angles

If you asked someone, "What's half of eight" and received the answer, "Zero," your first reaction would be, "That's nonsense."

But stop a moment. Think of the numeral 8. The figure is composed of two small o's — zeros — one piled on top of the other.

Take it further: If a line were drawn down the middle of 8, you would have two 3's standing face to face. From that perspective, half of 8 would be 3!

By taking a fresh look and seeing things differently, we can make all kinds of discoveries. We can replace old perceptions with new ones. We can combine old ideas in new ways and bring into being something which didn't exist before.

CREATIVITY
Frees imagination

New ideas and new approaches are all around us. Creativity is a matter of opening ourselves to possibilities.

In the 1700's, Londoner Jonas Hanway refused to accept the fact that he had to get wet when it rained. Having seen a tent-like contraption used in the Orient as protection against the sun, he adapted it for rain. The umbrella was born.

Frustrated by lack of funds for urgently needed housing for the elderly, a group of New England architects made apartment units out of abandoned buildings – a schoolhouse, a tannery, a convent and jail.

Stymied when volunteers failed to keep their commitments to finish painting the church, the repair committee chairman divided the surface into equal parts. On each section, in large, bold letters, he painted the name of remiss volunteer. The job was soon done.

Creativity isn't a matter of exceptional talent, artistic or other wise. As psychologist Abraham Maslow says, "A first-rate soup can be more creative than a second-rate painting."

"Now there are diversities of gifts, but the same Spirit. And there are differences of administrations, but the same Lord. And there are diversities of operations, but it is the same God which worketh all in all. But the manifestation of the Spirit is given to every man to profit withal." (1 Corinthians 12: 4-7)

After all, let's face the Bible fact; "God created man in HIS own image" DARE we deny that He EXPECTS us to be creative also?

MISCHIEF

Many people believe that Pastors are s'pose to be perfect. I doubt that the Pastors would agree. Some might pretend to be. Some might even believe they are.

Our Pastor had an elegant, dignified manner. He kept his whimsical side a secret, & acted business like & serious, most of the time. His sense of humor was always in good taste & restrained. His wardrobe echoed those traits, as did his office.

The trousers to the Pastor's new suit needed to be shortened. I shortened them. But, I used a very short six inch piece of red thread & sewed each leg together at the knee. No knots, just a loose connection that would come undone with the least bit of pulling. On the grey trousers it should show up quickly. I couldn't resist the urge to topple the Pastor's dignity, but it would be private, & make only him chuckle.

He decided to try the trousers on in his study, at the church, preparing for the next event. One foot in one trouser leg & it was stuck. Try the other foot in the other trouser leg. "What in the world is wrong?" he said out loud. Then, backing up & aiming for the nearby chair, he missed it & landed on the floor, with a thud. The table next to the chair toppled over. The secretary heard the noises & rushed into the Pastor's study without knocking, fearing for his safety, of course.

On the floor, sat the usually dignified Pastor in his shorts, with his legs stuck halfway in the grey trousers. What do you say at a time like that?

"Are you OK, sir?" she blurted.

"Yes, I'm fine"...he mumbled.

Just a second or two later, the red threads pulled loose, he yanked the trousers on & stood up, as the secretary rushed out the door.

She later admitted she didn't know if she should laugh or cry.

The Pastor emerged shortly, completely dressed, grinning & announced, "I owe Betty something...but I'm not sure what!" My mischief needed a response.

The next day he asked his secretary to devise a way to even the score. So, she brought an empty flat candy box, full of small stones, that she wrapped as a gift, fancy ribbon bow & all. She left it on Pastor's desk, intending to offer it as the "comeuppance" he was seeking, for me.

The secretary was quite new to her job & had not had time to become familiar with dates & schedules & stuff, so she didn't know that the next day was the Pastor's birthday. She ran down to get two cups of coffee from the kitchen, for their coffee break. Pastor got up so early every day, he appreciated her thoughtfulness.

As the secretary returned with a cup of hot coffee in each hand, she walked in as the Pastor had just unwrapped the lovely candy box...& opened it to find a box of stones!

Pastor laughingly confided to Bob & to me that mischief was something he had given up as a boy, & he never should have revived the urge. "BUT, Bob, your wife needs a sincere scolding!" he added grinning & patting me on the shoulder. TRUCE came as I sincerely apologized, & vowed to behave.

ARE FLAT TIRES BORING?

The Church parking lot was so full, that folks had developed sort of a routine for politely emptying this row before that row. It was neater &

simpler that way. But as I sat in my car, a friend, Peter said, "Hey, Betty...your right front tire is really flat, (only on the bottom, of course)" he grinned, then added, "But...I wouldn't recommend you drive very far. Maybe that station on the corner can fix it for you. Better not make any sharp turns tho'," he flippantly said over his shoulder.

My two kids didn't know about flat tires. They asked, "Mama, how will we get home?" They sat wide-eyed & troubled in the back seat. I assured them not to worry, as I examined that flat tire.

Our friend, Prudy, groaned, "I hate flat tires...they're such a bore!" She took one more last look at the right front tire, as she slid into the front seat.

Waiting our turn to exit the parking lot made me feel anxious. Prudy said calmly, "Father, we know that You have everything under control. That tire belongs to YOU. We all belong to You. Satan, shut up & leave us all alone! In the strong name of Jesus; and Father, lead us safely & quickly to the tire fixers we need, & meanwhile keep that tire healthy enough to get us there. In Jesus' wise & wonderful name, Amen."

We aimed toward the gas station on the corner, but suddenly chose to pass it by...& the next one also. As we passed them by, we discovered they were both closed. It was another block to the next service station, a block out of the way...not a logical choice. But...as we turned the corner, we rejoiced to see the AIR sign. An employee came quickly to the side of the car (full of helpless girls, he assumed) asking, "How can I help y'all?"

Prudy & I pretended to be helpless, to boost his ego. "Our right front tire is flat & we need your help!" we moaned, together, as though we had rehearsed it.

"You're joking, right?" he grinned. "Which tire did you say?" As he walked around the car a second time, Prudy & I got out to verify his strange attitude. He used his little tire gauge, checked to see that all four had the correct numbers & stood grinning, as if we really were joking. We finally filled the gas tank, so his time wasn't wasted, & drove off completely puzzled, but thankful.

Driving home the four of us began to sing, "Praise Him in the morning, Praise Him in the evening, & Praise Him as the sun goes down." As we laughed together, we once more thanked Him for His care, & His amazing sense of humor. How else would you describe it? It surely wasn't boring. And...once again...He did it!

That evening Bob came in & said, "Did you know your tire is flat?" & he fixed it.

OUR FAVORITE FIFTEEN VACATIONS

While my hubby was in the army during World War II, the army moved us more than 16 times between Texas towns...all on trains. Our possessions were packed in a four foot square wooden box, eighteen inches deep. It was so full that not one more safety pin would fit in. After four years, we returned to Michigan.

Our three children later learned, that visiting family, friends and National Parks all over the U.S. and Canada were their "mostest favoritist trips," when we were on trains.

All 15 trips started, as we drove two hours to spend the night with family on a farm, where the car lived for 32 days. Early the next morning we were taken to the first train (nearby) to begin the exciting adventure. After changing trains in Chicago, we finally landed in Whitefish Montana, where we usually rented a car for the thousand mile trip through Alberta & British Columbia, Canada as well as the glories of Montana.

When asked which is our favorite trip we can't decide between the gorgeous soaring mountains, the scary cliffs, the serene lakes, the lovely little towns, the big cities, the exciting six story waterfalls that splashed on us from a block away, the rocks bigger than our house, or the fabulous Pacific Ocean views. Thrilling photos galore cover most of the walls in our two story home, as well as the basement.

After returning the rented cars, we took more trains to visit friends...(some current, some from 60 years ago) and family. After another week in Washington, or Oregon, or Northern California, we took another train down the Pacific Coast near the "Big Sur," often stopping to visit Yosemite, the Red Woods, the trolley cars in San Francisco or Chinatown...plus many other fascinating places. We often wonder if the Rockies are more remarkable in our U.S.A. or in Canada. All of them are amazingly, breathtakingly beautiful. They just don't all fit in the camera. We really should buy another house with 20 rooms to hold all of the enlarged photos my husband keeps framing, & hanging...as friends say, "WOW! Where was that taken?"

The final week or two, were spent in Southern California with family members, who took us to fun spots like Disneyland, Knott's Berry Farm, the Tar Pits in LA., the Planetarium, etc, etc, ad infinitum. Then came the picturesque return trip through Grand Canyon, Arizona's amazing colors, New Mexico's mysteries, or the Colorado Mountains & gorges. Each time a different route, but all spectacular...and even educational!

Early training taught us to "Layer & Launder" what to take & what to leave at home. The biggest challenge always is...what did I put in which suitcase? I pack six. One large one, with warm weather stuff, goes to LA Union Station & waits there till we claim it. One small one gives us all clean things for the first leg of the trip on the first train in Michigan. Two more bags carry assorted items for hubby & me, plus the kids...for all weather & activities. The final two are TOTES, which contain sweaters, snax, books, games, & hard-soled slippers, for use on the train at night...and for all those daytime hours too.

Now, through smiles & tears, our adult kids & grandkids admit, the love of waterfalls & mountains, endless photos, & eating on trains and in the woods, is addictive. But...is it inherited or contagious?

IS THERE REALLY SUCH A PLACE?

My sister, Helen, & her husband Carl visited us many times from California. We tried to visit the lovely German restaurants & gift shops in Frankenmuth, Michigan, & the local zoo, gardens, & museums. But none of those things could compare to their mountains & ocean.

Once it rained nine of the eleven days they were here. They assured us they hadn't come to see scenery, they came to see US! If they'd wanted to see scenery, they'd have gone swimming in the Pacific Ocean. Besides, they were glad to see & feel rain...California is too dry. Hmmm.

On the next trip, Helen said, "You guys always tell us about your magic Mackinac Island. Why don't you ever take us there?" she paused, & teasingly added, "Is it really a real place, or did you make it up?"

"Hey, it's never open in April or October when you always come. Let's find out if there's any place open this early in May," I said.

We decided to drive the 200 miles to at least let them see the boats. At Mackinaw City the ticket agent tried to warn us. "It's not a good idea to go over without reservations. The last boat leaves the island at 8PM, so...be sure you find a place as soon as you get there, or you'll sleep on the grass in the park. Are you sure you wanta' take a chance?" he asked.

The look on Helen's face left no doubt.

Stepping onto the ferry boat, Bob & I placed our suitcases in the area set aside for luggage. Helen was reluctant to put hers down. "What if someone steals them?" she asked. Bob assured her, "This isn't Detroit or Los Angeles, dear...&...besides, if someone did steal your bag, where would he go with it? Toss it in the lake & float it to shore, perhaps?"

She laughed & set it down.

Carl got a big laugh at the dock on Mackinac Island, when he saw a bellboy from a hotel, on a bicycle, with seven suitcases piled on the front. How could he see around them? He couldn't!

Next to the dock, a Chamber of Commerce office is literally on the sidewalk, to help folks find a room. A dozen of the familiar ones were not open, not for two days or more.

"The Grand Hotel is open, but full, as it's their anniversary. Sorry, I don't see even one, that's open tonight. Better go back to the mainland & come back tomorrow. OK?" and she turned to her next customer.

We grabbed our luggage & ran back to the curb. Helen looked like she'd cry any minute. I told them to wait a moment, as I ran next door to the Murray Hotel. There were vacuum cleaners & stacks of sheets all over the lobby. The lady near the office nodded & motioned for me to come over to her desk. After she heard of our plight; I told her I had prayed that my California sister could spend time on our magic island.

"I can't promise, dear, but I know the folks who run the Haan House. Let's call them," the lady offered. On the phone they told us they would "open tomorrow," as many of the others had said. I took the 'fone & asked, "If I put sheets on the beds & scrub the bathroom, may we come now, so my sister won't go back to California without Mackinac Island thrills?" She laughed & said, "Awww...Comon'!"

One more answered prayer. Helen & Carl were shocked, when I told them the news. That was the moment that they understood why we warned them to pack light. Too bad they hadn't listened. The two men each carried two bags for awhile...but then I took my own light weight bag, so Bob could help Carl carry the heavy ones.

"Helen, no one would steal this bag, even in Detroit...it's too heavy," Bob quipped. Two lovely days on our sunny island, & Helen admitted we had not exaggerated in our descriptions. They loved it!

The day we arrived home, the sun hid & a storm exploded. Thank You, Lord, for providing precious memories. That was the last time they visited Michigan. Carl died the following year.

CAN MY ONE VOTE REALLY MAKE A DIFFERENCE?

In 1875 ONE VOTE changed France from a monarchy to a republic.

In 1876 ONE VOTE gave Hayes the U.S. presidency.

In 1923 ONE VOTE gave Hitler leadership of the Nazi party.

In 1941 ONE VOTE saved the Selective Service just 12 weeks before Pearl Harbor.

In 1649 ONE VOTE gave Oliver Cromwell control of England.

In 1776 ONE VOTE gave America the English instead of the German language.

In 1846 ONE VOTE brought Texas into the Union.

"All that is necessry for the triumph of evil is for good men to do nothing." – **Edmond Burke**

Pray. Find out all you can about the issues and how everyone involved feels about them. Ask God for wisom.

The Bible says to find some capable, godly, honest people who hate bribes, and...let them be responsible to serve the people with justice at all times.

WHAT SHOULD A CHRISTIAN DO?

1. Pray – Seek God's face and His Word as you actively cooperate with God's Spirit in living righteously. Then fervently pray for "all in authority. . . that we may lead a quiet and peaceable life" (I Timothy 2:1-2). Remember, "the effectual, fervent prayer of a righteous man availeth much."

2. Be informed – "My people perish for a lack of knowledge."

3. Register and Vote – Do it now and register others. Find out where the candidates stand on the basic moral issues of our day and the principles upon which America was built. Vote for the principles, not the party or person.

4. Rebuild — In your life and in others, rebuild God's message of repentance and right living; rebuild every American's responsibility to register and vote for the person who stands for righteousness. Rebuild the truth through proper information of the facts.

II Chronicles 7:14-15 "If my people, which are called by my name, shall humble themselves, and pray, and seek my face, and turn from their wicked ways; then will I hear from heaven, and will forgive their sin, and will heal their land. Now mine eyes shall be open, and mine ears attent unto the prayer that is made in this place."

THE FUNNEST DAY

The first 21 apartments & houses Bob & I lived in (during our first 20 years of marriage) were rented & so very temporary, that we never planted a garden. One place had grape vines in the back yard, so I tried to make grape jelly. My Mother told me how much sugar & how long to cook it, but she could not tell me how to keep my toddler & pre-schooler out of the kitchen; nor did she tell me that the grape juice that splashed on curtains doesn't wash out,...and the spots on wall paper are permanent. Too bad it had the wrong color flowers to harmonize with purple spots & splashes.

We tried a few times to plant some petunias, but had to move too soon to enjoy them. Gave up on that.

And then...we bought our new home in Saginaw & everything changed. We moved in March so, by May we got excited about the displays in nurseries of all sorts...every kind of flower, plant & bush.

Ron was about 13, Nadene was 17 & Linda was 4. We went together to go shopping. Each kid got to make some choices, & were thrilled to tell sleepy Daddy all about it. He worked 60 to 80 hours every week, & by the time everyone had showers & snax, he was more ready for bed than the kids were. But, he feigned excitement & agreed to see it all on Sunday. "Honest!" he promised. "After all, we can't see much in the dark."

On Saturday morning, after Bob left for work, a lady friend from church called to ask if we'd be interested in some of the things from her garden that needed to be thinned out & pruned. We were not just interested but eager. She told us to cover the back seat & trunk of the car with newspapers & bring bags & sacks for transporting things.

The excitement was so thick you could cut it! The kids couldn't find a place to sit...too many bags & newspapers. That sweet lady even gave Ron a small bag of Zinnia seeds plus plant food...the works! We took her a tray of cookies the kids had made the day before.

I can't remember all of the varieties she had ready for us. Our trunk was full & Linda sat on Ron's lap, cuz the back seat was filled with plants. All kinds of plants.

At home, the kids barely took time to gulp down their lunch before they started to dig & plant. Linda couldn't figure it out...especially the ivy sprigs that were "gonna' grow up the brick chimney." But she stayed busy handing the shovels & the big "Granddaddy Fork" to who ever needed them next. Giggles galore. We worked all day. I was glad there were leftovers for supper.

On Saturday, Daddy was always late getting home. His store closed at 9, but he couldn't leave till nearly 10 as they restocked & cleaned up. By then the three exhausted junior landscape experts were scrubbed & asleep. WOW!

Sunday morning, Daddy had left a note telling the kids he was too tired to go to church with them. He'd see them later. We tried to be quiet...but I don't think they really tried, they were sooo eager for Daddy to see what they had done.

In fact, Ron ran out to the back yard before breakfast to water all the new baby plants & especially the large circle, (about eight feet in diameter) where he had worked so hard to remove the sod, ever so carefully, & then found places to transfer it...to make a lovely zinnia garden, with the seeds the lady had given him. "They need water every day," Miss Marie had warned him & he took her at her word. In fact, he had watered three times in two days.

The kids couldn't sit still...they felt that church service would never end. They ran to the car.

As we drove in the driveway, Ron shouted, "Daddy's mowing!" BUT, his high energy drained, as he got a better look.

Bob was so pleased that the kids wanted to be involved, that he decided to rev up his engines too. In a large trash pile were stacked the ivy & other plants they had planted so carefully on Saturday. The only things Bob had not pulled out were the plants with flowers on them. "Oh, Daddy! What are you doing with our plants?" the kids shrieked.

"Well, I figgered you'd like me to help you," Bob said casually, adding, "I even planted some grass seed in a big bare circle in the backyard. Is something wrong?" Bob became aware there was a problem, & was totally confused.

As the kids started to explain, Linda started to cry and...poor Bob looked like he wanted to cry too. He had no idea what had happened, till Ron & Nadene took him to each spot explaining, as they moved from place to place.

Bob said, "Will you ever forgive your dumb Daddy for not only ruining your beautiful surprise, but also your beautiful garden?"

The kids hugged him, assured him of their love & forgiveness...and all four of them did what they could to remedy the major mess.

Then, Bob said, "Since I can't fix the zinnia garden that will be mowed like the rest of the grass...how's about, let's clear out another circle & put the sod back, on the one you dug out?"

Linda had no idea what was going on, but she helped whenever someone found a job for her.

A little later, Bob declared, "Hey, I've got an idea...would a picnic be about right?...Right NOW? Whoever gets washed up first hasta' put the tools away!"

"Hey Daddy, that's backwards!"

Bob agreed, "I know it. Let's have a backward picnic, even a backward day – the only thing we won't do backwards is DRIVE the car...OK? We even eat dessert first!"

That turned out to be a fun day...and...instead of the kids moaning & blaming Bob for the BIG mistake he made, & all their wasted work, time, & even Miss Marie's plants...they often referred to it as "the funnest picnic" ever!

SOME FOLKS ARE FIXERS

When my sister, Helen, & her hubby, Carl, visited us from California, it was fun to find new places to visit. One year we decided to drive to Holland, MI to see the zillions of tulips in bloom.

Bob had the car serviced the day before, as it was about twelve years old & he wanted to be sure no hoses would quit.

We packed overnite totes & left after a hearty breakfast. After driving about 20 miles, one of the little red lights on the dashboard began flashing.

Bob said, "Strangers wouldn't know what's wrong with our "beige beauty," so let's go back to our friend, Herb. He will know & he will be honest." So, we did.

Herb was very thorough; he thoroughly checked everything & said, "It's one of two things. I took care of the first one; the second would take a long time, cost a lot, & may not be necessary. If that's it, you can drive safely hundreds of miles before it fusses again. If that "idiot" light goes on again, tell it you're not an idiot & just ignore it till you get back home. Have a good time."

So, we left. No little light was on, and we felt assured that Herb was an expert.

After those same 20 miles, the little light blinked on again.

Helen said dramatically, "Bob, it's on again! What do we do now?"

Bob asked me, "Do you have an envelope in your purse?" Strange request. I didn't have an envelope, but I had a funny little bank envelope with bills from the check I had cashed. I emptied it & gave it to him.

Bob licked the tab & hung it over the wee red light, & spoke to it, "See ya' when we get back to Herb's place."

After a three day trip, Herb said, "What light?" It never did go on again. We sold the car two years later. That wasn't a miracle, but it was a blessing.

DO IT OVER AGAIN

Like many grandparents, we wish we had known then, what we know now, as we raised our children. To "do it over again"...if only we could...here are some of the things we'd change:

1. Those days & nights seemed 44 hours long. I wish I'd known how quickly they'd pass...&...that the next time I'd blink, my wee dollies would be graduating from high school.

2. I wish I'd spent more time hugging, hugging, holding, holding, laughing and cuddling them. I'd hold the bottle instead of propping it up, to create more permanent sweet memories, ignoring dust & dirty dishes.

3. Our adult son remembers the time I was cleaning the cabinet, under the sink. He sneaked up & yelled, "BOO!" It startled me & toppled me over, causing him to wonder if I'd call him naughty & be annoyed. Thank God, that time, we laughed & hugged, as he

presented his story book. I read it to him, sitting on the floor. He grabbed a banana, which we shared, before I put him in his crib for his nap. Had I known that memory would last; I would have tried harder to create more of them.

4. I wish I had praised & encouraged more, & scolded less.
5. I wish I had listened more & talked less.

But...I thank God for how He multiplies our loving attempts, & minimizes our failures, as mistakes of the head, not of the heart. God forgives us through the love of Jesus. We ask our children to forgive us all our mistakes. But, the hardest of all, is to forgive ourselves, since we cannot do it over again.

Cleaning and scrubbing can wait 'till tomorrow,
For babies grow up we've learned to our sorrow.
So, quiet down cobwebs, & dust, go to sleep.
I'm rocking my baby and babies don't keep.

SURPRISE!

When Bob & I were married in 1943, we had no idea that we'd still "like" each other & be planning a 60th wedding anniversary. Articles in newspapers and magazines, sounded helpful, but far too complicated...too much bother for our celebration..

We had discovered that life is more fun, & "easier to handle" if we kept things simple. So we chose to invite family, & a few close friends, to a truly simple event on Feb 2, 2003. It was nothing at all like those articles I had been reading. They were helpful & sounded lovely...but...I still preferred to have crackers & cheese & a fruit plate. Maybe I'd make cupcakes. That sounded simpler than trying to manage a big cake.

We got permission to use a room at our downtown church, & I started to sort through my tablecloths. Maybe I should buy a couple of paper ones...to serve about 25 or 30 people.

Then, our granddaughter made a startling announcement...NO...it was a loving, but firm command, a smiling command.

"Gramma, you & Grampa chose the date, & the time, & the place. We know what colors you like...and...you guys did the 60! So now, back off and we'll take it from here!"

We kept trying, but couldn't learn anything about the plans. It was all a big secret. Our son was sorry he couldn't make it here from

California for the event. Too much work. He told us that.

We were sooooo curious. We had Bob's blazer cleaned. I made a new jacket for my dress & cut my hair. What were those kids doing? No matter who we asked, we learned nothing. At one point, Bob asked, "Are you sure they didn't just forget? Should you make a few cupcakes, just in case folks show up and...well, I dunno'..."

One day, the Pastor asked if we'd like to renew our vows. Bob instantly & firmly said, "NO!...I meant it the first time!"

On Sunday morning, we were told to arrive at 5:30 p.m. When we did, we were "put" into a small room. We waited about 10 minutes, but it seemed like an hour. Then, our son, Ron, from California, walked in & laughingly urged us to not have heart attacks at seeing him.

As Ron ushered us into the large dining hall, music started & we were shocked...about 200 people from all over the country, stood clapping & laughing. I cried, of course. Bob waved one hand, looking like a triumphant politician, while holding tightly to me with the other.

Gorgeous turquoise, gold & white decorations looked professional, elaborate, and lovely; like Hollywood! A beautiful tiered wedding cake took center stage on a gold lame' table cloth.

The food on long tables looked like a magazine cover. It had taken days to prepare. We later learned that Ron had offered to send money to pay for the food, but couldn't resist the urge to BRING it instead.

Every table had candles & flowers & wee wine glasses for the alcohol-free wine, used later for a big time of toasting to LOVE. Old fotos mounted on turquoise cardboards, were on easels in several places.

Our kids had searched to locate music that was popular in 1943, like "Elmer's Tune" & "Three Little Fishies." Some of our talented musical friends led us in silly fun songs & then we sang "Amazing Grace."

To close, the Pastor brought the whole family together, and, as we held hands, he prayed for God's blessings & the true joy of Jesus on all of us. The room was filled with smiles & tears of joy.

Families can be filled with challenges, but they certainly are wonderful, and always full of surprises, memorable surprises, mostly happy surprises.

ROGER

A young man from Australia, named Roger, was WALKING across the United States. He had come to Saginaw to accept an invitation from a friend he'd met in College in England. I wonder if that friend ever believed that Roger would get to Michigan. It was Labor Day, a holiday, & he had stopped for breakfast at a local coffee shop.

My husband, Bob was having coffee with several of his cronies. They enjoyed their conversation with Roger, & then, they all left. Bob casually invited Roger to join us for a big picnic lunch at our house. Roger had tried many times to call his friend, & Bob assured him he could keep trying from our telephone. That was about 1986 BC...(before cell phones).

Everyone at our big lunch party loved Roger's charming Australian accent, & he also enjoyed our American accents & our American food. He told us we put the "em-PHA'-sis" on the wrong "syl-A'-bull." We had fun trying to discover & agree on WHO said WHAT correctly.

Roger's vivid descriptions of sheep shearing contests were fascinating.

It was difficult to listen to his exciting plans but not be negative about the wisdom & safety of accepting rides from strangers. His attitude toward America seemed a bit unrealistic, but we couldn't "throw cold water" on his plans. He kept calling his friend & got no answer.

Roger asked about the nearest hotel & planned to walk there. Bob & I insisted he stay in our empty bedroom. He only objected about 30 seconds before accepting.

His small suitcase, & few items in his pockets, surprised us. He had learned to "Layer & Launder" as we always did on our frequent 8,000 mile train trips. We offered suggestions about places in America we hoped he would be sure to visit. But, just walking the 200 miles to our beloved Mackinac Island seemed incredible, (& he couldn't even walk to the island).

We wondered why he felt he must do it in a year...& we wondered about his finances to "walk" from the Atlantic to the Pacific? But we didn't ask.

Because we had eaten early, I made a pitcher of lemonade & a big batch of buttered popcorn for the whole gang. Roger remarked, "Hey, I didn't know you could make this at home. I thought only big movie houses had machines to make it!"

He was also surprised that so many homes had washers & dryers...& glad to do his laundry here.

Just before bedtime Roger's friend answered the 'fone, & came to pick him up in the morning after breakfast.

Roger left lovely little gifts on his pillow for each of us. Two years later we received a letter telling us about the amazing places & things he had seen, and explaining that he had accepted some bus rides & train trips to complete his travels within the year. Then he told us the "rest of the story."

Roger's Dad had supplied him with the money, & a year to tour USA, so that he would then be ready to then learn to run their mammoth sheep ranch he would ultimately inherit. Roger was truly happy for the experiences & the treasured friends he had made. We exchanged Christmas cards for many years,...Blessings come in fascinating ways. We love the memories of Roger.

DISCRIMINATION

When I say discrimination, the first thing that comes to mind is RACE; black, white, red & yellow...and...that's not what I'm referring to at all.

Whether people are Mexican, Asian, African, Indian or European doesn't matter to me. I didn't include American in that list cuz usually Americans are mixture of several of the others.

When our church adopted a group of young men from Vietnam & Cambodia, they spent a lot of time with our teenagers. The group, seated on the floor, playing a board game, began to ask questions. "Linda, where are you from?" A Cambodian fella nicknamed Vit, asked of our teenager. "I'm from Saginaw," she answered. "No, I mean...in America, everyone is from somewhere else," he insisted. "Oh, I get it...you mean my ancestors. Well, I'm Mongrel," Linda answered, grinning & winking at me.

Vit frowned, paused, & pensively asked, "Is that from Mongrolia?" Linda showed Vit the dictionary and it took her awhile to explain that her background was English, French, German, Dutch, Irish, Scottish & probably Belgian. It puzzled Vit.

Then they all began to discuss the various attitudes around the world. In America, the people from Europe often seem to be more readily accepted than those from Asia or Africa or even Mexico. Skin color & language barriers too often dictate local attitudes. As their conversation continued, they discussed the early Asian attitudes of total isolation. Japanese, Koreans & others tried to eliminate all contact with "outsiders."

The one thing the whole group agreed on & emphasized ...

NO ONE wants to be the victim of discrimination. Not everyone understands the ramifications of that term. And...I believe it must be taught, it isn't natural to young children.

When Linda was four, a RACE was running to see who can get there first. She asked her brother, "What is a race riot?"

"That's when black people & white people fight & hate each other," he answered. "Wow, I never saw any white people & black people," Linda sounded amazed. "Oh! Silly, you're white & your Sunday school teacher is black!" Ron was obviously annoyed. "Ronny, that's not so! She's beige & I'm pink!" Linda was even more annoyed. "Always remember that Honey girl, & you'll do just fine," he smiled & patted her cheek.

Many years ago I was invited to do a short presentation in a large church with almost an entirely black congregation. The topic they assigned to me was WHITE POWER. As I prepared to share my thoughts, I asked many people their ideas of the topic.

A neighbor suggested, "I've heard a lot about GREEN POWER, money, but nothing else." My son offered, "The only white power I recognize is that pile of snow in our driveway!" A neighbor asked, "Is that a new washing powder?"

My husband Bob remembered that former President Dwight Eisenhower said, "Gun power, green power, black or white power...none of them are as powerful as true LOVE POWER which Jesus came to offer, & too many fail to recognize, let alone accept & use it."

None of us were sure of his direct quote, but I certainly agreed with the concept. Let's stop looking at color, except in flowers, autumn trees & peacocks, & develop the power of ONENESS of purpose. That was the balance of my message. I had felt very uneasy at the start, to be the only white person with only four other women in attendance. BUT...at the end, the entire congregation, clapped & stood, as I gave the Lord all the credit. He knew what needed to be said & used my mouth to say it. Praise the Lord!

Growing up in Detroit gave me a different attitude than many other people. We lived between a Jewish neighborhood & a Polish neighborhood. We learned to eat Polish kielbasa on Jewish bagels.

My Irish Gramma made German sauerkraut, French headcheese & Belgian dandelion wine for my French Grampa.

At public school I had a Jewish girlfriend named Mariam & a black girlfriend named Mattie (she called herself a Negro). Our next door friends were Italian & made great spaghetti.

After Bob & I were married in Detroit, he rejoined the Army in Texas,

& three weeks later I flew to Houston. I had to take a bus the 120 miles to Palacios, Texas. None of that seems unusual, BUT; it became my introduction to the true ugliness of racial divisions, via signs that said "Whites only" or similar bigotry.

As I got on the big bus with my suitcase, purse, & heavy winter coat (it was March & Detroit was bitter cold) I had to walk all the way to the back of the bus to find an empty seat. I sat on the very backseat...and then became aware that all eyes were on me...and...the bus was not moving.

The bus driver turned around, and...glaring angrily at me, commanded me in a loud voice, "Get off that seat so we can go on!"

I'm sure there were big racial problems all over Michigan too, but I had not personally encountered them. So, of course, I was shocked. I stood up for more than 40 miles on that bumpy ride, while holding my coat & purse.

At the next stop, we were told there'd be a 20 minute rest stop and, "Don't be late or we'll leave without you!"

At the door of the ladies room was a large sign "WHITES ONLY." A bit further down the hall was another sign, "OUT OF ORDER." Standing near it was a tall, handsome, nicely dressed black man, holding a tiny, adorable child, about two years old. She was silently crying with her sweet face buried in his shoulder. As I slowly approached, & patted her tiny arm, I asked her Daddy, "What can I do to help?"

That kindly, soft spoken black man said, "Thank you Ma'am...but...well,...she needs to use the rest room...I hate to take her in the men's room, but...well, you see the problem."

I extended my arms, she shyly responded, & I took her into the "White Ladies" rest room. A few ladies from the bus looked at me with disgust, but the sweet little two year old hugged me with gratitude, so it was OK.

That is, till we got back on the bus. A few people had left, so there were a few empty seats, but as I attempted to sit down, one lady placed her hand bag on the empty seat next to her. Another lady actually moved from her window seat & sat in the aisle seat, to prevent me from sitting next to her.

After trying four times, I finally was able to sit next to a young man who turned his face & wouldn't speak to me. I was tempted to return to that back row seat & see what the bus driver would do...but I just sat down & shut my mouth. That was my introduction to 1943 style Texas discrimination. Pain!

NOW, having said all of this, let me explain my REAL purpose for telling all of this "stuff."

I feel the pain of discrimination! I am a white, middle class woman living in a predominately white area of town. So, you ask...why do I feel discrimination?

Simple! I don't do .com. I have no email. I am a dinosaur. Many expensive prizes, (homes, cars, million dollar gifts) are available to....com. They assume EVERYONE has a computer. Those contests do not allow me to enter.

If I read a recipe or want to purchase a certain product, I must do .com to get needed data. If I drive to the pizza place I pay full price—but on .COM they get 50% off. WHY? Products & information are not available to me!

When I eat at certain restaurants, on their receipt, they ask what I think of their food & service. BUT, if I don't do .com no one CARES how I feel about their service & food. I don't qualify for their free awards, & I cannot enter their contest, or get their discounts.

Why not add a telephone number or address? Many of our friends (young & old) agree & they choose not to buy articles listed only on .com, etc.

Obviously, many companies don't care enough to include 'fone numbers or addresses for contact. They don't think the rest of us matter.

Years ago it was common to openly force folks to walk on the other side of the street if their skin was the wrong color. In some places that horrible, narrow attitude of intolerance & discrimination still exists, & takes many ugly forms.

Many folks will be annoyed at my sadly weak comparison. Truly this silly discrimination doesn't even compare to the other kind, but unfortunately it is rooted in the same self-centeredness & lack of consideration. I often wonder why some people care only about money...& themselves. I guess the cure is to get so busy helping others & 'doing good' that we can ignore those who 'DO BAD'

I'm sure there is good in computers.... But, it's sad to see that so much of today's technology can lead to addictive & even evil results. The Bible tells us to "OVERCOME EVIL WITH GOOD"—I keep wondering how to do that.

However, my blue-green eyes, and my no-longer-red-now blondy-beige hair color, or my white skin, are not what's causing me to feel discrimination. It isn't that I'm so poor that folks don't like the way I dress or look NO! The fact is I CAN AFFORD to buy a computer. Many of my friends can also...BUT we simply don't WANT to. Many folks have one, & don't like to use it...& resent the fact, (just as I do) that some folks assume that ONLY .com matters. I have a young friend who hates his computer & threatens to kick it. So, .com isn't first on everyone's list of values!

I guess it is pointless & silly of me to call it discrimination, but what is a better way to describe it?

NEVER STOP COURTING

Never stop courting; Marriage only gives you a chance to court without interruption.

Never let romance wane. The benediction at the wedding doesn't end romance. It only gives you a chance to be permanently romantic.

Never allow both of you to get angry at the same time.

Never talk at one another, either alone or in company.

Never speak loudly to one another unless the house is on fire.

Never find fault unless it is perfectly certain that a fault has been committed and then always speak lovingly.

Never taunt with a mistake.

Never make a remark at the expense of each other, it is a meanness.

Never part for a day without loving words to think of enduring absence.

Never meet without loving welcome.

Never let the sun go down upon any anger or grievance.

Never let any fault you have committed go by until you have frankly confessed it and asked forgiveness.

Never forget the happy hours of early love.

Never sigh over what might have been, but make the best of what is.

WHEN GOD CREATED FATHERS...

When the good Lord was creating fathers He started with a tall frame. And a female angel nearby said, "What kind of father is that? If you're going to make children so close to the ground, why have you put fathers up so high? He won't be able to shoot marbles without kneeling; tuck a child in bed without bending, or even kiss a child without a lot of stooping."

And God smiled and said, "Yes, but if I make him child-size, who would children have to look up to?"

And the angel shook her head sadly and said, "Do you know what you're doing? Large hands are clumsy. They can't manage diaper pins, small buttons, rubber bands on ponytails, or even remove splinters caused by baseball bats."

And God smiled and said, "I know, but they're large enough to hold everything a small boy empties from his pockets at the end of the day . . . yet small enough to cup a child's face in his hands."

And then God molded long, slim legs and broad shoulders.

And the angel nearly had a heart attack. "Boy, this is the end of the week, all right," she clucked. "Do you realize you just made a father without a lap? How is he going to pull a child close to him without the kid falling between his legs?"

And God smiled and said, "A mother needs a lap. A father needs strong shoulders to pull a sled, balance a boy on a bicycle, or hold a sleepy head on the way home from the circus."

God was in the middle of creating two of the largest feet anyone had ever seen when the angel could contain herself no longer. "That's not fair. Do you honestly think those large boats are going to dig out of bed early in the morning when the baby cries? Or walk through a small birthday party without crushing at least three of the guests

And God smiled and said, "They'll work. You'll see. They'll support a small child who wants to ride a horse to Banbury Cross, or scare off mice at the summer cabin, or display shoes that will be a challenge to fill."

God worked throughout the night, giving the father few words, but a firm, authoritative voice; eyes that saw everything, but remained calm and tolerant.

Finally, almost as an afterthought, He added – tears. Then He turned to the angel and said, "Now, are you satisfied that he can love as much as a mother?"

The angel shutteth up.

Erma Bombeck

TIPS FOR FATHERS

You gave your child a special gift, and by the way his eyes lit up when he opened it, you knew he was grateful. But when he set the gift aside, ran to you saying, 'Thank you, Dad!" and threw his arms around you – that's when your heart nearly burst with pleasure.

If that scene has ever taken place in your home, then you've witnessed a parable of how thankfulness can take us right into the presence of our Heavenly Father – and of the joy it brings Him when we come to Him that way. A truly grateful heart eventually turns its attention from the gift to the Giver. When we daily cultivate the seed of thanksgiving in our family, in time we will see the fruit of worship growing in them as they learn to keep their hearts sensitive and turned toward Him.

To worship God genuinely you have to know who He is and what He's like. Since no one has ever seen God, how do we know what He's like? The apostle Paul tells us that "God's invisible qualities — His eternal power and divine nature – have been clearly seen, being understood from what has been made" (Rom. 1-20). All of us – child and adult alike – first learn what God is like, and why He is worthy of our worship, by the things around us He has made, the gifts He has given us. If He made the mountains and the lightning, He must be powerful. If He made the sunset and the rose, He must delight in beauty. If He made the human body, He must be wise, and if He made the ostrich, He must have a sense of humor! Helping our children to thank God for His gifts, both great and small, will teach them who He is and send them running into His arms with grateful hearts.

Author Unknown

WHAT ARE FATHERS MADE OF? HERE'S A POEM THAT LISTS ALL THE IMPORTANT INGREDIENTS

A Father is a thing that is forced to endure childbirth without an anesthetic.

A Father is a thing that growls when it feels good and laughs loud when it is scared half to death.

A Father never feels entirely worthy of the worship in his child's eyes.

He is never quite the hero his daughter thinks he is and never quite the man his son believes him to be. This worries him sometimes, so he works too hard to try and smooth out the rough places in the road for his son who will follow him.

A Father is a thing that gets very angry when school grades aren't as good as he thinks they should be.

He scolds his son although he knows it's the teacher's fault.

Fathers grow old faster than other people.

While mothers can cry where it shows, fathers have to stand there and die inside.

Fathers have very stout hearts, so they have to be broken sometimes or no one would know what is inside.

Fathers give daughters away to other men who aren't nearly good enough so they can have grandchildren that are smarter than anybody's.

Fathers fight dragons almost daily.

They hurry away from the breakfast table, off to the arena which is sometimes called an office or a workshop. . .where they tackle the dragon with three heads – weariness, work, and monotony.

Knights in shining armor.

Fathers make bets with insurance companies about who will live the longest.

Though they know the odds, they keep right on betting.

Even as the odds get higher and higher, they keep right on betting more and more.

And one day they lose.

But fathers enjoy an earthly immortality and the bet is paid off to the part of him he leaves behind.

I don't know where fathers go when they die.

But I have an idea that after a good rest, wherever it is, he won't be happy unless there is work to do.

He won't just sit on a cloud and wait for the girl he's loved and the children she bore.

He'll be busy there, too . . . repairing the stairs . . .oiling the gates . . .improving the streets, smoothing the way.

Paul Harvey

"MY BOB"

It does seem that dating for two years & married for 69 would help two people to know each other. At least I thought I knew Bob. I'd like you to know him too.

He was clean, neat, loving, strong but gentle, efficient; silly at times, sillier at other times; the world's best Daddy; good at math, lousy at spelling, outstanding at his jobs in the army, & as a store manager plus supervisor of five large stores in five cities; excellent photographer; thoughtful of his parents, siblings & me; had a beautiful baritone voice; always well dressed with colors coordinated; a rotten gardener, a pitiful cook, an insatiable reader; never critical (his corrections were constructive & helpful); easy to cook for, courteous, 'generous to a fault'; an amazing sense of 'dry' surprising humor; Christ-centered in his words & deeds; and – a man of few words (usually the right ones). WOW! Does that sound like an all-around NICE GUY?

Our teenager once said, "Daddy's such a good boss at work, his employees treat him like God. He has to come home to find out he isn't." He grinned & chased her all over the back yard to give her a big hug & pretend slap.

Our other daughter once teased him about always being five minutes late. Not an hour, just five minutes. She grinned & teased, "Daddy, you're most unusual. While you're still alive, people call you the LATE Mr, Sharrer, but, as long as you 'get us to the church on time' – (not just for weddings) we will keep you!"

Just today I met a lady in a grocery store who remembers Bob as the best Sunday School teacher she ever had. That was 40 years ago.

In my first book titled "HE DID IT," I told stories about how God worked in our lives. One of those stories explained in detail how Bob had served four years in the Army Prisoner of War Camps in Texas. We were told that 'the half million German prisoners in the U.S. were the best kept secret of WWII.' After serving in other camps, Bob finally became Assistant Commanding Officer at Camp Swift P.O.W. Camp near Austin.

There were riots & murders at the other camps, & the murder trials were brought to 'Bob's Camp,' as there had been no troubles nor violence there. I won't go into detail again, (perhaps you read the whole story in my other book). I'm certain that Bob's cool courteous manner, (while he still demonstrated the firm authority that made the 3,000 German Prisoners & 900 Russian Prisoners obey & know that he was in charge), created that calm atmosphere.

However, God gave Bob the wisdom to use his gentle sense of humor, positive confidence, & respect for others, to treat all those prisoners as 'VICTIMS of War' just as we were. He kept them busy, after their hard work in the fields, using their skills & interests to fill their spare time, to prevent mischief & mayhem.

He allowed a truckload of POWs & guards to cut down cedar trees, which they used for many things. The Chapel they built for their own religious services, was covered with gorgeous hand carvings & had hand made altar & pews. They had no power tools but excelled with many types of hand work. A large cedar chest & hand carved chess set they made for Bob, are still amazingly beautiful. When Bob tried to pay for them, the men were insulted. They did accept hair brushes, & other trivia to keep Bob out of trouble with the 'Army Brass.' The hand carving of "Lt. Robert R. Sharrer" on top of the lovely box of chessmen is still a reminder of their skill and affection.

Because Bob's camp (as we called it) was peaceful, it became the model for others across the U.S. We thanked God when we heard there were no more murders in POW camps. We couldn't confirm it, but it was wonderful news anyway.

I've previously told you about Bob's lack of gardening skills, & we all agreed that the only things he could cook were a bowl of dry cereal, graham crackers dunked in a glass of milk, apples, & applesauce. When I asked the kids what Daddy gave them for lunch, they said, "Daddy told us to tell you we had a balanced meal; graham crackers & milk...an apple for us, & applesauce for baby Linda."

As for Bob's cooking skills...while he was still working long hours as manager of the large up-scale store, the three kids & I took a flying trip to visit lotsa' family in California.

Before leaving, we prepared meals for Bob's easy & quick late night suppers. We filled several divided trays with his favorite choices, covered them securely, labeled them with explicit directions for heating, & put them in the freezer. "Now he can set them in the oven & eat balanced meals quickly," we agreed, feeling very efficient & helpful to our 'hubby daddy,' as Linda called him. And we made a million cookies.

A week later, after many 'fone calls, Bob called again to ask, "What should I do with all of the casseroles & corn on the cob, folks have brought me?" We advised, "put those in the frig, & what about the corn?" It was dropped off three days before in a big bag. "Remove the shucks, & set the corn cobs in a pan of water. Then, cook them in fresh water for 10 minutes tonight, OK?" On to other topics.

In California we were all amused, but careful not to embarrass Bob. Later, he called to ask, "How do I light the oven?" We hadn't considered that possibility. Back home a week later, as we unpacked our bags, I took a quick peek in the freezer to inventory those 'quick meals.' They were all still stacked neatly, just as we had left them – and – on the bare shelf next to them, sat four 'naked' ears of corn. "Bob, why are those ears of corn staring at me in the freezer?" I asked. "Well", he answered, repressing a grin, "after I did manage to get the leaves off, I put 'em in a bucket of water & forgot them. Three days later, they smelled bad, & the trash man had just left, so I had to figure out what to do with them for a whole week till he came back again...sooo...my only choice was to put them in the freezer till the trash man comes next week." His voice trailed off, his head down & then he burst into a big grin & said joyfully, "Since I never ever could turn that oven on...& you know how, let's have those meals for supper tonight, OK?"

Handwriting was never important to Bob, & after signing his name 7,000 times every hour at work, his writing got worse. Truthfully, it was awful. Mail that came to our home had at least 30 different spellings for our last name. Our kids found it amusing at first, as they each learned to read & write their own name. Later it became a constant source of teasing As he returned home each night, they'd call him by the name on the current mail; "Hello Mr. Shaver" or "Hello there Mr. Saucer!"

Bob never lost his sense of humor, and a few times he asked ME to bring in the mail. I agreed. But, the kids ran across our busy county road faster than I did. "Sorry Mr. Snover, we beat Mom to the mailbox," they smirked.

When Bob did arrive home after those 12 to 14 hour days, he found joy & relaxation in pulling our son around the block on a sled at 9 p.m., or building a snowman together. The frantic giggling episodes of learning "Chopstix" on the piano; or the help with homework, were treasured by our kids, and later by our grandkids. One of Bob's favorite 'relaxers' was to walk all over the house with our grandbaby snuggled up close to his face, singing into her ear, "Zero, Zero, Zero with sugar on it" over & over & over. She obviously loved the sound & vibration of his deep soft sweet voice. When we asked what he was singing, he told the other kids & me, "I'm singing sweet nothings to my dolly." She snuggled even closer. The other kids remembered he had done the same to each of them, & they all loved it...and him.

One evening Bob acted unusually tired & quiet. I asked why, & learned that his boss was acting like a "gold-plated jerk." I offered,

172

"Let's us agree that he's stupid & doesn't know how valuable you are to him. Then let's tell him to, 'TURN BLUE, you big dummy'. Let's say it together...one, two, three"...and we did say it together, as we laughed & hugged each other.

Then Bob said, "I'm too tired to sleep, so let's just open a can of peaches." He went to the basement for a big can of store-bought peaches & we ate peaches till the can was empty.

Most men have some knowledge of cars & lawn mowers. Bob didn't. After he put in the wrong mixture of gas & oil (or whatever) and fouled up the lawn mower, our son-in-law announced, "Hey, if you want me to mow your lawn, just say so. It would be easier than making me fix it after you mess it up!" So they laughingly compromised, Bob would mow, but Rod would 'feed the beast' & keep the mower 'mowable.'

Because he worked such long hours, I tried to find ways to help Bob with ordinary tasks, so I offered to take over the checkbooks. We had two, because I had the alteration business called "SEW SPECIAL" in our basement, & taught classes at Delta College & Jo Ann Fabric Store. Bob was pleased with my offer. The first few months worked out well & the checkbooks balanced. Hooray! Numbers were never easy nor fun for me, so it was a great effort... but, if it helped Bob, I was glad. OOPS! The checks starting popping like pop-corn, & I was stunned! We had been writing checks on the wrong account (or sumpin' like that???) & I was ashamed that Bob had to figure out why they were bouncing. He was amused...I was not. He smiled, hugged me, & said very sweetly, "Hey, let's be glad it worked for a while & was a big help to me. Now, let's admit that you are a much better COOKER than I am, & I'm a much better COUNTER than you are."

Bob was the oldest of six. His two younger brothers & three younger sisters depended on him till it became silly at times. After they were all married & moved apart, one evening Jeanie called & shouted, "Bobby the grass is on fire!" He calmly answered, "Jeanie, Call the fire department! I'm 100 miles away...get everyone to safety quick!" We all laughed about it later, but not that night.

Bob, & his entire family, were nutty about cats. As a boy, he trained one to sit on the piano, near a doorway, & bat her paw at everyone who entered that door. His Mom said he wanted to prove that cats can be trained, to dispute the claim that it's impossible. He bragged that no cat would train him! But, when Buttons knocked Grampa's hat off, Bob was told to retrain or punish the cat. Instead, Bob moved the piano, claiming it was a better place for it anyway. He had taught the cat to be so naughty, that they put her in the bathroom while everyone was away from home. They were all shocked to find that Buttons had unrolled the toilet paper, & emptied the entire medicine cabinet into the wash bowl. Their Mom asked, "Bobby, shall I punish you or the cat or both?" So, he kept that naughty cat in his own bedroom. His brothers complained, but Bob found the whole episode comical.

In 1984 while I was at a Christian Women's Conference in another city, our daughter became very ill. Her 19 year old daughter & 14 year old son were worried about her, of course. When I returned, I wasn't surprised to see what Bob had done to help Dan. After they had prayed & heard their Mother was improving, Dan was restless & still worried. So, Bob decided that he & Dan should set up the train. That seems simple till I explain, that the track went in & out of each of the four bedrooms, & down the long narrow hall. There were black streaks of oil & hand prints on every wall & every other surface.

As I arrived, Bob winked at me, to try to prepare me for the awful mess. It didn't really, but because I knew to trust Bob's motives, I kept silent & laughed with them as that long, smelly, noisy train puffed smoke & whistled in & out of every room & down that long hall. It seemed to help, as Dan & Bob worked on it all day. Bob had taken the day off cuz Dan needed him. Bob later painted the walls. Big job!

Speaking of walls, all of the walls in our house, (that's first & second floors, plus basement) are covered with lovely photos that Bob took on our 8,000 mile Amtrak trips, through mountains & gorgeous National Parks. Bob admitted that he was "addicted to trains, mountains, cameras & kids"...then, he'd grin & add, "and music & cats." Those amazing trips took place about every two years for decades. We never stopped thanking Bob for thinking of them, to show us such breathtakingly beautiful places, and for bringing them home with him, in his camera. Many people told Bob his photos were better than those on calendars & in magazines.

For Christmas & birthdays, our kids & grandkids gave Bob boxes full of frames (14" x 17" & larger) they had found at rummage sales, etc. Of course our family & friends now have walls covered with lovely photos too. Often when folks came to visit, Bob would take them to the basement to "claim their photo." He started, to cleverly place his incredible, carefully framed photos, one on each wall, but soon decided that 37 of them on one wall looked even better. The nail holes that he fought at first, are all covered with beauty now.

What we never understood was, how Bob could work 60 to 80 hours every week, all year long & still find time to take care of our two cars, mow, or shovel snow, enjoy our three kids, (& discipline them at times,

174

in his own style) & still be a good husband? Our neighbor once asked Bob, "How do you rate 30 hour days & nine day weeks? The rest of us haven't figgered out how you do it & still keep smiling."

Bob just grinned & snidely answered, "Well, football & baseball aren't at the top of my list, but I just might move golf up there if I could play as well as you do. Ya' know, I don't need 30 hour days, just 25 hours would help me make up for all the times I'm five minutes late."

Whenever we were driving around, Bob managed to get lost. It became a big joke to everyone. One daughter said, "Daddy needs me to be his navigator; he gets lost coming out of the closet." Bob reminded us that he flunked map reading in high school & in the army; "That's why they made me an officer, so they cold assign me a driver." Then he'd grin, pat me & add, "I've heard that real men never ask directions so...I'll agree to stop the car at the gas station & buy some gas, if you'll agree to ask directions, OK?"

Because of Bob's reputation for getting lost, many of us gave directions that he didn't need. Often it was teasing by our kids, & Bob never lost his sense of humor...but...one day he turned to me, as they were overdoing it, & asked, "Do you have a screwdriver in your purse?" "No,...why?" I was puzzled. "Oh, I just thought I'd take off this steering wheel & hand it to our backseat crew."

Several years ago Bob decided our daughter, Linda, needed a dependable car, so he would drive to California to give her ours. He then decided to drive to & through Whitefish, Montana to visit our son, on the way. Each time he called I thanked him & urged him to call again every other day, so we'd know that he hadn't turned the wrong way to end up in Canada.

On the target day, I was delighted that Linda called, "Mom, I can only talk a minute while Dad brings his luggage in, to tell you he found me, G'bye!" A few minutes later, Bob called & casually said, "I only got lost twice, & they weren't serious." We considered it EPIC that he made it across the continent alone, & didn't drive into the Pacific.

Because I grew up in such a poor family...(we didn't KNOW we were poor tho' cuz all our friends were too) we really learned to count our pennies, literally. Bob truly laughed when my Mom paid $1.00 a month on each of our bills so they'd not write us nasty notes to collect the remainder of the $50 or $90 we owed. So, I grew up seeking bargains.

But, Bob taught me a good lesson. I needed a new baking pan & planned to buy the cheapest one. His rule was, "Will you use it often...like once a month? Buy a better one....Once a year, the cheapest....Once a week...buy the best, when it's on sale, or at the cheapest bargain store." It still works for more than pans. Thank You, Lord!

Birthdays were always a problem, cuz Bob could never remember them. None, not even his own. But, he found a solution that was not only workable, it turned out to be wonderful. At a date, somewhere between the big holidays & other notable events, Bob brought home exciting & surprising gifts, wrapped beautifully, & he would say, "Happy UNbirthday," with a great flourish & fanfare. It truly developed into more fun & was more notable, cuz it made us all realize he had thought of us when it was not expected.

When it came time for Bob to retire, business men & store owners coerced him to help them out, temporarily, & he retired five times. Then it came as no surprise that he opened three dry-cleaning shops, which were successful. But, one day he announced, "I've worked long enough. We're never gonna get rich, so let's sell them all & then play awhile." So, he did...& we did. He spent endless hours framing his lovely photographs & listening to his music. The kids teased that his taste was limited to anything called music, from Beethoven & Bach to country western, to organ recitals, to Elvis Presley, to "Jesus Loves Me" & everything in between, including the "1812 Overture."

He even took up golf. His last few years were truly play-full, & great fun. But, then Bob's illness required more care than I could give him. We were grateful for the tremendous help & blessings we received from V.A. Hospital. The staff & doctors were kind, efficient, thorough & treated him with sincere respect. They were always good to me too, & cared for him for a month, so I could visit my 95 year old sister & our two kids in California.

Then he needed more care, & at the fine nursing home, he became 'their favorite patient.' They gave him double desserts every day. One nurse said, "Bob doesn't have a sweet tooth, he's just sweet all over!"

At Bob's funeral, our grandkids chose to use some of Bob's fabulous photos on the notes & folders supplied by funeral homes. They set up large easels to display more of his gorgeous mountains scenes all over the room. It was very impressive, & would have pleased Bob. He would've calmly said, "Better to show God's glories than dumb pictures of me."

I hadn't realized that during the last few years of Bob's life, as I spent 29 hours a day, ten days a week caring for him, how I had truly neglected the entire house. Some folks asked me, "How could you take care of Bob so long?" My answer was easy, "Because he was so sweet & easy to care for. He just smiled & cooperated. Even when he couldn't talk & could hardly walk, he carried dishes to the sink after every meal." Everyone was amazed at his gentle strength & constant good humor. One young boy told us he "saw Jesus in him." Bob cried when he heard that, & shook his head, "Oh! No...not me."

When I started to clean out the closets after we put my dear Bob to rest, I found some surprises, that I'll tell about later...but first, after I placed his sox, Pj's & all of his clothing in boxes & bags to donate, a lady said, "You're certainly not giving away all of Bob's beautiful clothes, are you? I'd hate to see some dirty old derelict wearing his lovely things. And, you surely want some things to remember him by, won't you?"

I was shocked! My answer was not as gracious as Bob's would've been. "Our entire house is filled with the wonderful photos Bob took of all the trips we took together, & the paint on the walls we chose together. Plus our kids & grandkids...why on earth would we need his clothing for remembrance? I pray that everyone who gets them will be blessed, in the name of Jesus!"

I then felt ashamed for being so abrupt. When I apologized, she said she forgave me.

After Bob moved to Heaven to spend Christmas with our young daughter, his three sisters, two brothers, all of our parents, and Jesus, I decided to really clean out all of the dresser drawers that held his 'private stuff.' I do admit, I learned a lot about Bob that I didn't know.

In the back of Bob's sock drawer, I found his coin collection. He had told me he saved old coins, & planned to show them to me, but we both stayed so busy, that we forgot.

A good friend located the catalogs & prices, & then found a buyer for all those precious, valuable coins. The friend chose to buy one for his daughter whose birth date was on one of them. Bob would have been pleased.

In another drawer, I found a shoebox full of postage stamps. For many years, we had all helped 'unglue' & save lotsa' stamps for Bob's collection, & that was no surprise. BUT, the big shock was on the bottom of that box. It's hard to describe the enormity of the shock.

There were many long envelopes, that had yellowed with age. They were postmarked 1938 & 1939, from faraway places...all over the world. Belgium, Zambia, Switzerland, Italy, Fiji, plus islands & remote places that I had never even heard of! The outsides were fascinating, but not as remarkable as what we discovered inside each envelope.

At the age of 17, Bob had written to the foreign embassies in those remote & enchanting places, to tell them he was a stamp collector; would they please mail him some stamps (either post marked or not)...& they did! Some of the envelopes had extra stamps inside. Many thanked him for the $1.00 bill he had included with his request. Such a treasure.

Also, in the bottom of that box, were many old postcards. Some from 1902, 1910, 1927, etc. Bob obviously had begged them from family & friends. I recognized a few names.

We were all amazed that, at 17 he had the initiative & the ability to seek addresses for all those embassies & official sounding offices, to learn the required amount of postage, & then write such 'adult' sounding letters. All of this stuff didn't just amaze me, it brought all of us to tears. We agreed, if we had done all of those things we would have bragged about the success of the project! Wouldn't you?

Our son had decided years ago to collect stamps, so it was easy to choose the future of Bob's amazing collection. Our admiration for his brilliance & determination never diminishes. We wonder how many of today's 17 year old boys/men would go to the great trouble it took to locate the data & pursue the project. That was before computers, and information was not so easily obtained.

As I continued to sort Bob's trash & treasures, I found manila folders (stacked up about 7" high, & buried). Each one had the basic name address & fone number, of an employee...but Bob had added other facts, such as personal color choices, taste in clothing & jewelry, food preferences, etc. plus, he had listed the accomplishments & improvements of each of the 80 ladies & one man who called him BOSS. I can't imagine the other managers, of the 42 stores in that chain, going to the trouble of using that data for the holiday events & monthly birthday parties Bob planned. It's no wonder that Bob's store surpassed all others in goals set and achieved every year.

Years before when the BIG boss had offered Bob a large store in downtown Detroit at double the salary...they were all bewildered & shocked at his refusal. He said, "I'm honored that you considered me for that big store, (& even bigger salary), but, no thanks, I do not want my son to learn how to handle a switchblade, so, we'll stay where we are. Thanx again." Can you imagine their reaction? I was glad that our son meant more to Bob than money.

After Bob's elegant & impressive military funeral at the National Cemetery, we were on the way to the memorial service at our church about 50 miles away, when our grandsons ordered (on cell fones) several chocolate Frostees from Wendy's. At the church they divided them up into small paper cups & invited everyone to join. They reminisced, "This was Grampa's 'favorite fruit' he gave each of us Frostee sips before we were a month old, & regularly after that, so we salute you, dear Grampa. We love you forever."

We're told that God created men to need to be respected, and women need to be loved. I'm thankful that I married a man who deserved my respect, and, that I knew he loved me. I'm grateful for 72 years with such a fine, strong sweet man. Linda called him a 'marshmallow in a gorilla suit.' He often introduced me as his first wife. He claimed he 'raised me from a pup'...& tried to train me his way; that failing, he tried things my way; that failing, we then agreed to let Jesus show us THE way.

I often called Bob 'my favorite husband.' I am glad that together we learned that Jesus said, "I am the way, the truth, & the life. No one comes to the Father but by ME."

Bob is with Jesus now, & I plan to join him there...I wonder when, – But, as Bob often said, "I'm not in any hurry."

DRINKING FROM MY SAUCER

I've never made a fortune
And it's probably too late now.
But I don't worry about that much,
I'm happy anyhow.

And as I go along life's way,
I'm reaping better than I sowed.
I'm drinking from my saucer,
'Cause my cup has overflowed.

Haven't got a lot of riches,
And sometimes the going's tough.
But I've loved ones around me,
And that makes me rich enough.

I thank God for His blessings,
And the mercies He's bestowed.
I'm drinking from my saucer,
'Cause my cup has overflowed.

O, Remember times when things went wrong,
My faith wore somewhat thin.
But all at once the dark clouds broke,
And sun peeped through again.

So Lord, help me not to gripe
About the tough rows that I've hoed.
I'm drinking from my saucer,
'Cause my cup has overflowed.

If God gives me strength and courage,
When the way grows steep and rough.
I'll not ask for other blessings,
I'm already blessed enough.

And may I never be too busy,
To help others bear their loads.
Then I'll keep drinking from my saucer,
'Cause my cup has overflowed.

MY WISHES FOR YOU...

I wish you a shaft of sunlight on the gloomiest of days.
I wish you a long, lazy morning with breakfast in bed.
I wish you the sound of your children's laughter.
I wish that no matter how much it rains, your socks never get wet.
I wish you a kiss in the moonlight from someone you love.
I wish you patience, because sometimes the world will insist on walking when you want to run.
I wish you the abandon to dance badly at weddings.
I wish you a good memory, except for grievances.
I wish you rainbows and fireworks.
I wish that no matter how venerable an age you attain, at least once a year splash in a puddle.
I wish that you never fear failure, for doing so makes it hard to succeed.
I wish that you're never the last to laugh.
I wish you a mountain to climb, and the will to do it.
I wish you passion.

I wish you the vision that lets you see good in others and the faults in yourself.

I wish that you know where the fuse box is whenever the lights go out.

I wish you heroes.

I wish that no matter how tall you walk, you never look down on those around you.

I wish you the strength to face your fears, to recognize them as part of yourself, and still move on.

I wish that you find your own path through the forest.

I wish you courage.

I wish you laugh lines, not wrinkles.

I wish you the sense to laugh at the world and all its absurdities, and the wisdom to laugh at yourself before others do.

I wish that you can feel my hand in yours whenever you need it.

I wish you a home as welcoming as a mother's embrace.

I wish that you see that beauty lies in the shadows as well as in the sun.

I wish that you always have one wish left.

Author unknown

LIFE'S SEASONS

There's a season for beginnings
when the world is fresh and new,
when we shape our dreams
of all the things
we plan and hope to do;
A season for maturing
when we think and work and grow;
And a season for the harvesting
of all we've come to know.
And each successive season
grows still richer than the last
as treasures of the present
add to memories of the past.
Katherine Austin

THE HAPPY MOOD

It's lovely, and it's mine, and I shall not
expose it to the wind, the weather or
world's comments; in a green-edged corner
of my heart I'll enclose it with mist and
moonbeams...and it needn't make sense!
Florence Jacobs

HISTORY

The whole topic of history was boring to me in school. But, when we began to travel around this amazing country, "history-came-to-life" literally. As a result my two books have had spurts of my story, and HIS-STORY, blended with the words & stories of many others. That's where I seek, & often find, fascination; the pure delight & thrill in the lives of people who didn't run scared. I'm haunted & amazed by the successes that could have been failures. That's the joy I love to roll-around in history.

Some of history jolts us, shocks & alarms us; some calms us, assures us; and some is truly amusing. I recently learned about the Frenchman we call Cadillac. Much of Detroit's history revolves around him. Folks honor & deeply respect his role in the early days of the straits that he named "de troit" – (troit means strait) – But, I've learned that he had changed his own name, & when Detroit folks sought to honor him in Europe in the place of his birth... he was not highly respected there, & barely known. So history very often surprises.

What will history say about us? What are we really made of, deep down inside?

Are we wimpy & allowing our lives to be boring as we drift along? Or do we find tenacity when we need it, to bring excitement & exhilaration? It's easy to give up, to give in, & admit that scary things happen. At times we may need to appear crazy (maybe we need to act crazy)!

Visions & dreams are so fragile that we can watch them float away, or be crushed, or lose luster, just by being so sensible. We can become an ugly kind of negative without even knowing it. A passage in the Old Testament calls complaining & murmuring a sinful prayer. Ouch!

So, years ago in my sewing classes at Community Centers, the YWCA, YMCA, and Delta College, etc. I introduced my pupils to a

"Negative Nickel" jar. Anyone who said anything negative had to put a nickel in the jar; & everyone became an enforcer. Usually one person said, "With my luck I'll hafta' bring a pocket full of nickels!" I assured them, "No, I'll have a supply – but put one in now to start us off." "What happens to the nickels?" they asked. "Hey, I hafta' listen to the nasty negatives, so I get to keep the nickels!" was my answer. There were times I had to put my nickels in, too. But, at the end of the series of classes, I bought them a bag of candy to remind them "How sweet it is to NOT be negative."

Thirty years later, I was stopped in a mall, by a former pupil, who remembered my name, & loudly announced, "My family had a "Negative Nickel Jar" for years, but due to inflation it has now become a "Quarter Can," AND it still keeps my five kids & us more positive!" She swung me around, hugged me, & ran down the hall with her grandchildren.

Let's not overlook the impact that sillies, & even wild ideas, can have all around us. Are great accomplishments created only by great people? Or does an ample supply of grit & grace & determination & love & creativity, & even fantasy, produce the greatness?

I've heard we should limit the "shouldn't" & the "can't" so we don't dilute the joy of progress, even when it comes only a penny's worth at a time. Gratitude and praise produce better results than blame & shame do.

Let's not search for spiritual highs or extraordinary mysteries & stuff; let's just snuggle down & enjoy HIM in the ordinariness of every day, as the light of Jesus' love bathes our lives.

Our history is full of folks who...well, Alexander Graham Bell could've given up when folks laughed at him. George Washington could've decided it was too cold, his men had no shoes, and there were too many Red Coats on the horizon. Thomas Edison could've quit when he failed some 900 times. Jonas Salk could've believed there was no cure for polio. Michelangelo's arms must've gotten tired. Helen Keller had every reason to quit, but she didn't. Marian Anderson & George Washington Carver climbed walls of Racial hatred, but they didn't quit. Ludwig Von Beethoven could've quit when he lost his hearing. Franklin Delano Roosevelt became President with Infantile Paralysis. Abraham Lincoln over came abject poverty & lack of formal education to become President. Marie Curie didn't listen to the men who were sure no woman could...but she did it anyway. Those folks didn't let the hurdles block their path. No timidity.

Back to the historic tale we've heard of a silver-tongued orator named Edward Everett who spoke with gestures & eloquence. His speech lasted an hour & 57 minutes. Then Abraham Lincoln was introduced. We're told that he spoke in a high pitched, almost squeaky voice, without moving, when he spoke those simple words, "The world will little note, nor long remember ..." BUT truly, those simple words will never be forgotten! His Gettysburg address lasted two minutes; and, he didn't need eloquent pauses nor dramatic gestures...it came from his heart.

If we celebrate & re-remember the years behind us they become stepping-stones of strength & joy for the years ahead

I have no idea who wrote this, but I must share it:

If we cry, we may appear sentimental;
If we laugh, we may appear foolish;
If we hope, we may risk disappointment;
If we try, we may risk failure;
If we show feelings, we may risk exposure;
If we reach out to help, we may get too involved;
If we love, we may risk not being loved in return.
If we write, we may risk ridicule!

So, let's decide to cry, to laugh, to hope, to try, to show feelings, to reach out to help, to love, and to write ANYWAY!

THE CENTER OF THE BIBLE

This is pretty strange or odd how it worked out this way. Even if you are not religious, you should read this.What is the shortest chapter in the Bible? Answer: Psalms 117. What's the longest chapter in the Bible? Answer: Psalms 119. Which chapter is in the center of the Bible? Answer: Psalms 118. Fact: There are 594 chapters before Psalms 118. Add these numbers up and you get 1188. What is the center verse in the Bible? Answer: Psalms 118:8.

Does this verse say something significant about God's perfect will for our lives? The next time someone says they would like to find God's perfect will for their lives and that they want to be in the cener of His will, just send them to the center of His Word!

Psalms 118:8 "It is better to trust in the LORD than to put confidence in man."

Now isn't that odd how this worked out (or was God in the center of it?)

MAKE DO

Growing up on the heels of the "Great Depression"taught us some simple tricks that supplied our needs...for finances and dignity. No one told us we were poor. If they had, we wouldn't have believed them. Thinking back, the innovations were endless. It was 1933, and we learned how to *make do*.

Dad's vegetable garden was the size of a bathtub. Exaggeration? Let's say the size of a double bed. His carefully placed seeds used all vertical and horizontal spaces. Neighbors traded seedlings assistance, advice. Mom washed the precious veggies over a big bucket, which later watered the garden. Daddy used dandelion's for salad, wine, and comfort. Long before crop rotation became popular, Daddy, who could barely read and write, rotated, staggered, and fertilized his meager crops to "get all the good stuff outa' the ground."

My sister Helen (at 12), planted flax seeds and cooked the harvest to make a slimy mixture she used to set the neighbor's hair. they loved it. Shampoo and set...10 cents...haircut...25 cents. At 13 she made dresses for me. I was 8 years old. We learned to alter the cast-off dresses the neighbors discarded. Mom washed clothes on a washboard for us and others too. Later she got a washer that rinsed clothes in the bathtub. We were 15 and 10 by then, so we ironed, mended clothes, shortened curtains, skirts, and slacks to earn nickles and dimes from neighbors. We found a throwaway hand-push lawn mower to earn more dimes. At the end of the month we were delighted to buy rock salt for the handcrank ice cream freezer--and pay the light bill.

No surprise that Helen became a professional beauty operator washing and ironing her starched white uniform every night. Neighbors gave us their outdated Sear's catalogs to cut out pictures of ladies and kids in their underwear. Old fabric scraps and colored paper (from ads) made clothing for my paperdolls. Flour and water paste glued them to cereal boxes. Mom carefully opened bills and letters, saving envelopes for paper doll wardrobes. A paint store gave us old wallpaper books to make placemats, birthday cards and paper doll clothes. Some folks consider recycling a new idea. It was the theme of our lives. We never heard of rummage sales – we used everthing beyond it's normal life. Adult coats and jackets with worn out sleeves and collars made great coats, skirts, and pants for kids. After patching the patches on adult pants, we cut them off to make shorts, pants or vests for little kids. Now folks pay extra for pants with holes. Lace borders from worn out pillow cases made collar and cuffs for a new blouse. Sock dolls and scrappy quilts brought joy (still do!). Even scraps of soap were boiled down together to use in the washing machine.

The edges of worn out towels made great bibs, and washcloths. We split worn out sheets and sewed edges together in the center. "Sale" bed sheets make the best tablecloths, napkins, and placemats. No ironing needed. We couldn't buy toys, so we begged a huge box from a furniture store and drew on it the face of a big clown. By cutting out and removing the eyes, nose, and mouth, we created a fun game. Neighbors stood in line to take turns tossing hand made bean bags through the holes. Points earned stirred great competition. We kept score in the dirt with a big stick.

Our dad drove a huge truck that helped repair overhead wires for the Detroit Street Railways. After two weeks of long hours (often overtime) he proudly brought home his check for $10.00!!! Big Detroit was close to bankruptcy and schools closed early.

Mom's soups, stews, and biscuits were famous. From her we learned to use things in the fridge that "must go"...but never were boring leftovers. We still get rave reviews for some of them.

The sewing classes and "Creative Banners Workshops" I've taught at 3 colleges, several community centers, and fabric stores are all the direct and exciting result of those early years of learning to _make do_ with what we had. Creativity and techniques we learned through necessity, have become blessings – not only to ourselves, but to countless others (...and wages besides).

With all the technology available everywhere, will kids ever learn the fun of counting the rings that surround a pebble dropped in a big puddle of water? Or lie on a grassy hillside with a friend and decide together if those clouds look more like a bunny or a bear? Inexpressable joy comes of learning to _make do_; and so did our lifelong careers.

THE EXCHANGE AT THE CROSS

1. He was punished	..1. that I might be forgiven
2. He was wounded	..2. that I might be healed
3. He was made sin with my sinfulness	..3. that I might be made righteous with His righteousness
4. He died my death	..4. that I might share His life
5. He was made a curse	..5. that I might receive the blessing
6. He endured poverty	..6. that I might share His abundance
7. He bore my shame	..7. that I might share His glory
8. He endured my rejection	..8. that I might have His acceptance
9. He was cut off from the Father	..9. that I might be united with the Father
10. My old man was executed in Him	..10. that my new man might be alive in Him

Let your pen show all of the contours of your life and personality, and – trace the delicate embroidery of the unexpected, the creatively gorgeous stuff. Maybe you or I can't "clasp the shadows," but let's try to learn the difference between those folks who – when they're on a train, they see the poles and tracks and yawn.

Some great writers told us about those poles and thought of the trees that these once were in a forest. Some folks wrote short stories about the people on the train. Some wrote essays – I've heard that an essay prompts us to want to discuss, or even argue with the writer. I was told my "Wit & Wisdom" should be called "Mirth & Moralities", well, whatever we call stuff, let's try to invite folks to discuss, even if they disagree – in fact, that's often more interesting.

CONCLUSION

Now, we've reached the end of all the quotes & clever ideas I've collected; some of which may have bored you, but hopefully some amused you as much as they did me. Actually, I find a few of those quotes interesting no matter how often I read them. Abe Lincoln's stuff is both witty & wise, and timeless.

You & I are not apt to say or write anything that folks will quote 150 years from now...but, let's not squelch our urge to use creativity, the sweet sensitivity, & the joy that gives us reason to remember, to cry, to laugh, to enjoy, to share...and yes, to write.

Today may be full of lotsa' good stuff, & probly' yesterday was too; the stuff that others will enjoy reading about someday. The hopes & dreams that make our tomorrows glisten, will be built upon, & fed, & nourished, & deeply enriched by our memories. How can that happen if we don't write them?

If this 91 year old retired sewing teacher, who can't even type, (and...the main thing I know about computers is that they can't shorten pants)...could write two books...what is holding YOU back? I'd love to read YOUR stories, which will become YOUR STORY!

——AND, if you ask God to help you, in Jesus' name, He surely will. I asked Him...& HE DID IT!

CPSIA information can be obtained
at www.ICGtesting.com
Printed in the USA
FFOW03n1206030618
47037638-49328FF